ASCENSION

Divine Stories of Awakening the Whole and Holy Being Within

Enjoy these other books in the Common Sentience series:

ANCESTORS: *Divine Remembrances of Lineage, Relations and Sacred Sites*

ANGELS: *Personal Encounters with Divine Beings of Light*

ANIMALS: *Personal Tales of Encounters with Spirit Animals*

GUIDES: *Mystical Connections to Soul Guides and Divine Teachers*

MEDITATION: *Intimate Experiences with the Divine through Contemplative Practices*

NATURE: *Divine Experiences with Trees, Plants, Stones and Landscapes*

SHAMANISM: *Personal Quests of Communion with Nature and Creation*

SIGNS: *Sacred Encounters with Pathways, Turning Points, and Divine Guideposts*

SOUND: *Profound Experiences with Chanting, Toning, Music and Healing Frequencies*

Learn more at sacredstories.com.

ASCENSION

*Divine Stories of Awakening the Whole
and Holy Being Within*

Featuring

WILLIAM HENRY

SACRED STORIES
PUBLISHING

Books may be purchased through booksellers or by contacting Sacred Stories Publishing.

Ascension: Divine Stories of Awakening the Whole and Holy Being Within
William Henry

Print ISBN: 978-1-958921-01-2
EBook ISBN: 978-1-958921-06-7

Library of Congress Control Number: 2022948529

Published by Sacred Stories Publishing, Fort Lauderdale, FL USA

CONTENTS

PART THREE: DEEPENING YOUR ASCENSION EXPERIENCE

MEET OUR SACRED STORYTELLERS
MEET OUR FEATURED AUTHOR

PART ONE

Understanding Ascension

The knower and the known are one.

—MEISTER ECKHART

WHAT IS ASCENSION?

ho am I? Where did I come from? What am I doing here? How do I live the best life while here? Where am I going when I leave—and most importantly, how do I get there?

These questions have been asked for millennia, on Earth and likely elsewhere.

The answers are complicated, but also simple. They could be reduced to one sentence for each question.

The quest to find these answers triggers our natural spiritual abilities for transformation and evolution, both as individuals and as a species. Transformation leads to a sense of wholeness, holiness, and completion that changes our bodies, raises us beyond human, and enables us to "walk with the angels" in the sacred realms.

This is Ascension.

The ascension quest is rather like the search for the Theory of Everything equation, which vexed Stephen Hawking and eluded Einstein for the last thirty years of his life: the elegant, one-inch equation that summarizes all the physical laws governing this universe we call home.

Pursuing this equation is the job of some of the smartest people who have ever lived. They study things we can't see (subatomic particles) that make up all the things we can see (matter). Some of them believe that the destiny of all life in the universe depends on answering this call and solving this equation. Discovering it will take humans from having the "theory of *almost everything*" to complete knowledge about the universe—or *universes*, as it is likely that the layers of the universe might be like the layers of an onion, and the number of layers might be infinite.

The people asking the above spiritual questions, and those asking the physics questions, are on parallel paths.

Like the physics gurus, the spiritual ascension masters have sought to condense their teachings of the ages into "ascension equations" or practices that are simple to follow. One of the oldest of such equations is this:

"Loving God with all your heart, mind, and soul and loving your neighbors as yourself = self-realization and Ascension."

This equation answers most, if not all, of the questions above. It makes the essential point that moving away from separation, hatred, and ignorance and toward higher, self-less acts will benefit all life.

With this ascending path comes the emergence of a consciousness and a higher intelligence that is cosmic, mystic, and practical in that it enables us to scale new heights. I call it *angelic* or *ascension intelligence*. Tapping into this ascension intelligence or ascension consciousness empowers us. Some even believe a better human will bring about the ascension of our entire home planet. As these answers are sought and discovered, a new being rises and emerges from within us.

We ascend. Earth ascends. Heaven rejoices.

Ascension means rising. It is an action that implies climbing and realization, especially self-realization. This is why—in addition to the bridge, rope, and tree—the ladder is a most apt metaphor and symbol for Ascension.

One does not simply ascend a ladder. One climbs it. The ascending soul must learn to rise, grow, develop, transform, transmute, and *climb* into the heavens.

As we will explore, many traditions tell us that this ladder is not "out there." It is "in here." Our precious body, itself, is the ladder. We are to learn to use it, as well as to discover all we can about who provided this ladder to us.

The spiritual goal of transcending the material world and uniting with the Divine in the spiritual realms beyond might be humanity's oldest desire. It could be called the Theory of Everything of Spirituality. While the theory of everything might answer the question of who created all this, the ladder addresses the question: "How do I get there, and where did all this come from?"

Certainly, it's not in your flesh-and-blood body. Our bodies are garments or suits that are worn while we're on Earth. You can't take it with you.

Well, maybe you can.

Your Ascension journey might culminate in you becoming a meditation master adept at rearranging all of those invisible, subatomic particles that make up your physical body and transforming them into a radiant body made of pure energy, into which your consciousness is deposited.

Attaining this body of pure energy is the ultimate outcome of Ascension. From this perspective, Ascension is two things:

- One, it is the awakening and raising of consciousness and a quest for wholeness, holiness, and completion.
- Two, the transformation or perfection of the body from its material, solid, flesh form into higher, subtler light body form that is capable of living in the higher regions beyond the Earth, which are inhabited by supernatural beings.

Metaphysically speaking, Ascension is as much about unfolding, evolving, developing, and disclosing this new "light" being within as it is about rising. In actuality, a better word is *revealing*. The light body is not something we retrieve or turn into. It is already present within us. Turning into light is actually turning inside-out, which reveals what is hidden within our lives. In Ascension, our outer matches more closely our inner.

It is important that we realize this sooner rather than later.

As we will see, the spiritual goal of transcending the material world—and uniting with the Divine in the spiritual realms beyond—is an ancient desire. But it is also our most imperative current need, as immense technological and geological forces are challenging us. From artificial intelligence to climate change to the threat of global war, our time is filled with anticipation and peril.

Ascension involves a complete change in identity and lifestyle. It is a transformation of one's entire life…which takes us beyond the perils of Earth life.

Raising vibration is often spoken of in relation to Ascension. This is a raising above the distracting, lower impulses, actions, and thoughts. The objective is not to remove these desires as much as it is to direct our desire toward that which is good or godly. As the soul's desires come into attunement or alignment with God's, it is able to activate its fuller capabilities.

The goal of raising one's vibration is to see the Divine more clearly and to allow the Divine presence to be experienced more fully and sweetly. When the soul ascends, it can see, hear, and feel from a higher vantage point that brings new light and wisdom about the self and the world.

Enfolded within each of our bodies is the ability to ascend and to transform. What we see when we look in the mirror is a fraction of who we truly are and what we can become, if we commit fully to completing our Ascension.

Along the way, we must be open to change and willing to accept that as we change our outer self, our inner self changes, too.

A key analogy for our journey is the acorn.

It is hard to comprehend the growth, unfolding, or ascension process of the oak tree that rises from within the acorn. We might be astounded by the potential enfolded within that tiny seed, hidden within the nutty enclosure, to produce a glorious tree—and not just any tree, either. The little seed becomes a massive oak—a tree that is considered sacred or holy the world over.

The completed form of the holy oak is within the mundane acorn, but one would never know it. The acorn and oak tree look nothing like one another. Not until the right conditions are provided does the acorn's genetic coding, and destiny, kick in, and the transformation begins. Then, the whole or perfected holy oak rises from the soil.

The venerable oak has been revered as a symbol of strength, resilience, power, wisdom, longevity, generosity, and Divine spiritual connection. These are all attributes and benefits the ascension quest provides the awakened soul. Hence, the acorn is a wonderful metaphor for Ascension.

Nothing happens with the acorn while it is hanging in the tree. It must take a journey into the lower world and be planted into the ground to find its potential.

So, into the ground we go.

THE ROOTS OF OUR ASCENSION

Spiritually speaking, Ascension has been the core objective of religious practices for thousands of years. The concept of Ascension is based on the belief that our souls do not come from Earth, but rather, we were planted here. It includes the idea that there exists a higher realm, a source reality from which we originated—as well as a means to return there. To get there, humans must transform and ascend.

Exactly *how* to do this is not clear.

While the spiritual concept of Ascension is found in the world's major religions, it is often misunderstood or unacknowledged. It might be because, like the roots of a tree, the concept of Ascension—and even more, the teachings about how to do it—are buried underground or "sub rosa" within the exoteric or traditional teachings of religions. Sometimes, Ascension is even the most secretive aspect of the tradition.

Consequently, awakened souls are left to find the way upward on their own. This requires stopping for a moment as we wander the forest to examine a single tree. It might be a book or a story that catches someone's attention and puts them on the ascending path. It might be a story about a ladder, a stairway, a rope, or even a portal. The book or story might become the tool itself. Often, these tools are provided by an otherworldly source. God might be the one offering you the book.

Prior to the 21st century, if an average person knew about Ascension at all, it likely came from references in the Christian Holy Bible. They probably also thought it was something that only happens after one is dead.

Wait. *Can* one ascend while living?

Most definitely.

The book of Genesis enigmatically says Enoch "walked with God" (Genesis 5:22-24), implying that he ascended in bodily form. Elijah ascended in a fiery chariot. Jesus ascended in front of witnesses, including two angels dressed in white. In Catholic tradition, Jesus' mother Mary was the first Christian to ascend to heaven. The Gnostics say Mary Magdalene ascended. The apostle Paul ascended "to the third heaven" (2 Corinthians 12:2).

But the Holy Bible is not the only source of ascension stories. Six hundred years later, Mohammed ascended upon his lightning horse, Al Barak, during the Mira or Night Journey. And St. Francis of Assisi's ascension in the 13th century is one of the most astounding stories of all.

In each instance, God reached out and activated or enabled ascension while the person was alive. In each instance, there was also a secret teaching that activated and motivated the ascension, transforming the subject.

In Christianity, Ascension is a literal, bodily return to heaven and emergence into the presence of God. As Jesus will return the same way he left (Acts 1:11), it implies that the ascended body is different from our physical form. It is a return to our original, light body form. This is why Jesus is sometimes shown in a cosmic egg, wearing the garment of light, in Christian ascension art.

Various higher planes or otherworldly locales, sometimes called *celestial cities*, are detailed in ancient ascension texts. These include *Sion* or the *New Jerusalem* (Jewish/Christian), *Vishnuloka* (Hindu), the *Pure Land* (Buddhism), *Shambhala* (Tibetan), and *Field* or *Dimension of the Blessed* (Egyptian). All are populated.

Entrance to these locations is accessed via portals or gates. Entering these portals or gates requires that we are dressed appropriately—as I say, in our robes of light.

Many of these episodes refer to one-way ascension journeys taken from Earth to another region. But in some cases, the ascended ones return to Earth. It is immensely beneficial to follow the stories of those further along on this path.

Are there more stories? Other types of ascension journeys? Oh, yes. Many more. Ascension is not only an ancient pursuit—it is ongoing. It is happening now. In fact, there has never been a time in history when so many people were actively working toward, or living, their ascensions.

We are fortunate to be alive during a time when ancient accounts of one- and two-way ascensions—and the knowledge long buried within these stories—have found their way to the surface. These works reveal that, in the ancient mind, the boundary between heaven and Earth was once viewed as crossable, just as it is becoming today. Immortality was possible by ascending to heaven. From pharaohs to holy men and women, to Roman emperors, ancient literature is filled with stories of humans who found the ultimate secrets and fulfilled the ultimate quest. They left keys for us to follow.

We will explore their stories, and seek their keys, as we go.

MY STORY / OUR STORY

I have been on the ascension path for more than thirty years. While I didn't set out to become an ascension teacher and historian, or even a conscious ascender, I gradually became one, and my path continues. This journey has been a series of ascension awakenings.

When I was eight, I made my bewildered parents stop the car during a family vacation in Wyoming so I could stand in the middle of meteorite field. Another time, I was called over to and zapped with a profound impulse of love by St. Francis of Assisi's cloak while visiting the church dedicated to him in Assisi, Italy. I have always felt nudged by something to go, see, do, feel, and study things that led to my realization. By tracing a few of the steps along my path, we can blaze a trail to more fully understanding Ascension and its possibilities.

In 1988, I was twenty-six years old and living in Nashville, Tennessee. I had spent the previous six years studying whatever I could about everything from Gnostic Christian mysteries to neuroscience. Then my interest turned to the question of angels and extraterrestrial intervention in human affairs in the ancient world.

One summer evening, a friend invited me to a screening of a documentary about Billy Meier, a Swiss man who claimed to have had interactions with a beautiful woman from the Pleiades, the spectacular star cluster that many ancient cultures pointed to as their place of origin.

Meier offered an extensive collection of astounding photos of what he alleged were alien spaceships. He called them "beam ships." These photos were so amazing that many people, including me, wondered if they were even real.

While driving home that night, I looked into the clear, star-lit sky from my convertible, and something quite simple, but extraordinary, happened. My reality shifted. For the first time, I saw the stars not as two-dimensional points of light on a black background, but as 3-D worlds with vast distances of space behind them and with life inhabiting them. I saw all those dots of light we barely give a glance to as the rotating orbs of life that they are. This moment was like a pebble being dropped into a pond. As my new perspective rippled through me, suddenly, I had an emotional connection to a living cosmos that had not been there before. I wanted my car to turn into a beam ship.

My inner reality changed at that moment as my heart and mind embraced my rapidly expanded outer reality. If you put your hands out in front of your shoulders with your palms facing one another, that would characterize my consciousness before this moment. Now, if you open your arms as wide as you can, that characterizes me afterward. It was as if the universe just went "whoosh." The gate opened.

In that moment I *knew* and *felt* life out there. Moreover, I felt connected to what was "out there" and "in here" for the first time. In and out became one. It was tremendously exciting.

As the wheels in the kaleidoscope of my mind turned, I felt the bits of my soul awaken, jiggle, and reorganize into a new pattern or belief system. I didn't know it then, but that moment—that first, small step in awareness— was a giant leap on my ascension path.

I have often reflected on this moment. Why had I never seen the cosmos like this before? It could be that I simply never paid attention, at least not consciously. I had looked at the stars many times, but until that night, I had never seen them. I had to wake up to see the stars.

Later, I had a similar moment of awe when I saw the Milky Way arching across the sky for the first time while I stood on a mountain in Aspen, Colorado. You and I live on the outer arm of an enormous, celestial disk. Beholding this disk from a dark site, its core radiating like a flaming heart sprinkled with billions of stars, presents a wondrous river for the soul to explore. We have only just begun to discover all that is "out there."

ALL THAT IS

My recognition of my place in the universe, and the accompanying awakening or ascension of my consciousness, was a micro version of the galactic awakening astronomer Edwin Hubble prompted with his discovery of the expanding universe. Did you know that, until 1926, humans believed we lived in a celestial egg, and that our Milky Way galaxy was the entirety of the universe? All that is, we believed, was what we could see.

That's right. Until 100 years ago, humanity thought the entire universe was comprised of only the stars we see in the night sky. That's it. Then Hubble began looking at photographs of the night sky that showed cloudy patches called *nebulae* or interstellar clouds of dust. Most of Hubble's colleagues at the Mount Wilson Observatory thought these fuzzy blobs of light were all *in* the Milky Way, but Hubble didn't think so. Could there be anything *outside* the galaxy?

Hubble answered the question by taking the best possible photos of these fuzzy things and proving that they were outside and beyond the Milky Way. The cloudy ball of light was a whole different galaxy!

We named this newly discovered galaxy number two, *Andromeda*.

Hubble's discovery led to the realization that our galaxy is a sister galaxy to not just a few, but more than a few hundreds of billions of galaxies that inhabit the known universe. I say *known* universe because some scientists believe we live in a multi-verse. Hubble also proved that our universe is expanding. This realization led scientists to seek the physical origin of the universe.

Suddenly, Hubble's answer to the fundamental questions about our existence—*Who are we and where did we come from?*— rose to a profound new level of understanding.

By increasing the size of the known universe many, many times over, Hubble took us closer to the soul's true garden and origins. His discovery cracked open the cosmic egg. This was humanity's great awakening. Our collective ascension had begun.

We now know that our galaxy is one of 100,000 galaxies in what is called the Laniakea supercluster of galaxies—but this is only a tiny fraction of the universe. *Laniakea* is a Hawaiian word meaning "immeasurable heaven."

It never ends. It is calling to us.

As a believer in reincarnation, I offer that our souls must go somewhere when we are not in the body. So, where do we go? Where were you before you came to Earth, this time around? Where are you going from here? Have you ever thought about this? I know I have.

The very idea of "life between life" suggests we have been returning to physical form, again and again. Many believe that our soul evolution is decided prior to incarnating into another physical lifetime. As people and situations enter our lives, we might begin to understand that we pre-selected these experiences before we incarnated, to assist our soul's growth and ascension. Do you believe that? How many times have you solidly, irrefutably, recognized or experienced this?

Our souls must be able to navigate the afterlife—but where is this place we call the afterlife? It's out there, but where? How do we get there?

These are ascension questions.

The afterlife realm is really the in-between life before we incarnated as humans. We go round and round in between and into lives. How do we escape this merry-go-round? We ascend. We realize the merry-go-round is not horizontal. It is vertical. It is a spiral. The goal it to ascend this spiral.

THE OLDEST ASCENSION STORY

The goddess Inanna, the Queen of Heaven, goddess of love, and daughter of one of the Anunnaki gods, is the hero in the world's oldest ascension story, "The Descent of Inanna Into the Underworld."

An astounding statue of the goddess from ancient Syria is evidence that Inanna might have been an ancient astronaut. Discovered by French archaeologists in 1935, this human-size statue shows Inanna wearing an extraordinary helmet and a majestic robe, among other Divine objects.

The helmet is called the *shugurra* helmet. The Sumerians said this word meant "the Crown of the Steppe." Literally translated, *shugurra* meant "that which makes go far into the universe."

I was awestruck and mesmerized by this statue. What kind of a helmet can one put on that makes them go far into the universe? I wondered. I was enamored by the possibility that Inanna came to Earth to show humans how to join her in the netherworld.

Her robe, the *pal-a* or miracle garment, also played a role in Inanna's ascension. I was utterly transfixed by the idea of a garment that somehow enabled her to perform miracles. To me, Inanna was telling us what to do and how to do it so we could join her.

This robe, which is composed of wavy lines and covers her body, is called the *melammu*, a Sumerian word that means "Divine radiance." Wearing this robe gave the gods a supernatural, awe-inspiring sheen, a glow of whiteness, light, and spiritual force. The radiance is a distinguishing attribute of the gods, one that separates us and them. The *melammu* gave the gods superpowers, making them "giants" or "mighty ones." However, the Anunnaki taught that this garment is transmittable. A human can become a "mighty one" or giant by acquiring the *melammu* from a Divine being.

The Anunnaki are described as humanoid, but also luminous, radiant, or shining beings. They radiate rainbow-colored light. Hence, they are called the Shining Ones. Their luminosity was attributed to the *melammu* cloak or garment which they wore while on Earth.

According to the Sumerian texts, the Anunnaki came from, or descended from, the heavenly realms. They can return or ascend to their realm at will, via this cloak. If one wishes to have dinner at the Anunnaki table in the celestial realms, one must be dressed appropriately.

I can't promise you a seat at this table. However, by learning about this wondrous robe and connecting it to numerous ascension traditions, you will accelerate your own ascension. I can promise that by the time you finish reading this book, you will have a pattern for this cloak and tools for weaving it.

As for getting a dinner reservation, you are on your own.

GOLDEN SOUL / GOLDEN ROBE

Atra-Hasis, an 18th century B.C. Akkadian epic, is one of the earliest ascension texts. It describes that in a quest to create a "servant of the gods," Enki—the god of wisdom, smith craft, and magic—along with his female companion goddess, Nihursag or Ninti, modified a primitive human species (*Homo erect-us*) by putting on it "the image of the gods." As described in the Sumerian tablets: "The newborn's fate thou shall pronounce; Ninti would fix upon it the image of the gods; And what will be is Man." *Atra-Hasis* says they did this so the new being could tend the garden of the gods.

What is this "image?" Was something overlayed upon us? Something that we can take off or remove? Like a robe? These questions have perplexed scholars.

Some believe the image of God relates to our unique cognitive abilities. We know that many animals have intelligence and feelings. Social media is loaded with videos of animals displaying compassion and emotions that humans possess and can learn from. But there is a gap, a huge gap, between what animals do and what humans do with their intellect. The Book of Genesis argues that this is because we have the image of the Creator. Animals don't. Many speak of a "ghost in the machine" that separates us from all the other creatures on Earth. We have the "ghost/image," and animals and machines don't.

We also have an enormously powerful neocortex that was mysteriously activated by some unknown means around 200,000 years ago. It is quite startling to realize that neuroscientists cannot explain how the part of our brain that makes us human—that enables math, science, art, and all human civilization—was activated. Some believe it was not by a natural process. Someone, or something, fused two chromosomes into one and made us human.

The primitive human that resulted from his handiwork is called a *Lulu*, "the one who has been mixed," meaning it is a blend of human and otherworldly DNA. All of this knowledge of genetics was summoned to make a better gardener or gold miner.

Interestingly, Enki was also an alchemist and the higher, actual, goal of alchemy is to turn our leaden soul into a golden one through a process of self-purification or self- realization.

Was Enki actually here for souls? Was he "mining" souls? Why not?

The term *alchemy* was applied equally to the human soul as well as material elements, like metal (lead), and components as earthy as the human body (clay, mud). The goal of both Ascension and alchemy is the same: the *perfection* of the elements. Gold-making is god-making. Gold symbolizes humankind's quest to perfect, illuminate, and refine itself and live as a golden being in a golden age.

Also called "the Work," alchemy was practiced by the Sumerian, Egyptian, Greek, Essene, and the first Christian mystics as a Divine and sacred art of transformation, regeneration, and resurrection into a body of light *like* the gods (god-making). This "body" of light is symbolized by the robe of light, the *melammu*.

Alchemists learned a lot about the nature of our soul by comparing it to gold. We can, too. Technically (and alchemically) speaking, gold is a soft, shiny, yellow, heavy, malleable, ductile metal. It is also a trivalent *and* a univalent, which means it is a *transitional* metal. As a transitional metal, gold is symbolic of flexibility on our spiritual path while life experience galvanizes our faith. The golden halo in art is the symbol of the soul glowing from within.

Because of its resistance to heat and acid, gold is a symbol of *immutability*, eternity, and perfection in all matter, on any level. In Christian symbolism, gold is considered an attribute of *virtue*.

Seeing ourselves as in a transitional phase—being flexible, virtuous, and aimed at perfection—are golden mental attributes on our way to ascension. With these attributes we are weaving our golden robe.

From my perspective, it is clear that the reason why the human body was altered was to be a more conducive vehicle for the ascension of the soul. It was then that I realized this story, told in poetry, might be more than just a parable for the purifying and ascent of the soul. It might be telling us what happened.

FIRST HUMAN, FIRST ASCENSION

These masterful stories reveal that after the first human (named Adapa) was created, Enki infused him with great wisdom. Adapa became an adept. However, Enki withheld immortality from him.

In the *Myth of Adapa*, we read that Enki took the human to the otherworldly throne of the Anunnaki high god, Anu, to display his handiwork to the Anunnaki Divine Council. In order to reach Anu's throne, Adapa left the boundaries of the earthly world, walked through Divine travels, and mounted his way to the highest heaven. He was escorted by Enki. As the myth says:

He (Enki) made him take the Path of Heaven, *and he went up to heaven.*
When he went up to heaven, drew near the gate of Anu.

Adapa clearly ascended from the Earth and was taken up to heaven. Sumerian art portrays Adapa ascending with streams of light coming from his body.

Enki, who was also a trickster god, feared that Anu was going to offer Adapa the food and drink of eternal life. If this happened, Adapa would be transformed and made equal to the Anunnaki. This implies that the human body of Adapa would have become like the luminous or radiant body of the Anunnaki.

Enki realized that if humans were so empowered, he would lose status; the emperor would be revealed to have no clothes, so to speak. Or worse, his creation might turn on him. So Enki told Adapa he should refuse any food or drink offered by Anu, because it would be the food and the drink of death.

As this story unfolds, Anu was shocked that a human would refuse a direct path to immortality and equality with the gods. No matter, he gave Adapa a robe and anointed him with oil and returned him to Earth, where he resumed his mortal life. According to the Assyrian references to the wisdom of Adapa, he composed a *book of sciences* titled *Writings regarding Time; from Divine Anu and Divine Enlil.* Adapa, thus, is credited with writing mankind's first book of astronomy, the calendar … and Ascension.

ALMOST ASCENDED

Adapa's story is the beginning of all human quests for ascension. The point of the story is that Adapa *almost* ascended. While he went up to heaven, he did not stay there. He came back down. His was a two-way ascension journey, rather than a one way trip to immortality.

For millennia, humans have been told this story in one form or another. It has been repeated in many languages. For example, Adapa is easily seen as a prototype for Adam in the book of Genesis. Why has this tale been repeated? What makes it so enduring? And why is the message twisted? Why couldn't the story- tellers tell us, straight up, whether we can or cannot ascend?

Apart from the fact that the gods can be tricksters, within this story are three ascension take-aways:

- One, there is a boundary between Earth and heaven, and not everyone can cross it. Adapa was allowed to go up to heaven, but did not stay. The rest of us must be invited to that realm; otherwise, we are viewed as intruders. If you have ever heard the phrase "storming heaven," it is a reference to this message that there is a boundary separating the earthly from the Divine that humans must "storm" to cross over.
- Two, we became earthbound as a result of this teaching. The purveyors of this story also taught us to identify with our fallen, "almost ascended," earthly selves rather than our immortal, Divine selves. Who am I? Earthly? Divine? This identity crisis is at the heart of our search for *something* more while enjoying our earthly experience. We know we are meant to go somewhere, but do not know how to get there. Some of us give up seeking this, but…

- Three, this story tells us the gods have a secret something—a plant, the food and water of immortality, or a robe of light—that enables us to ascend. Adapa refused these gifts.

Henceforth, Ascension and immortality has been denied to all of humanity…or at least, all of those who do not seek it. However, clever humans *can* discover these secrets. Many have done so. The secrets are in the stories.

Why haven't more of us sought the secrets? It is because of how we have been taught to view ourselves by millennia of spiritual and religious indoctrination that basically says, don't bother seeking. You can only ascend once you're dead. Even today, religious teachers will tell you Ascension is only possible once you are dead. This was a trick used by the ancient priests. It safeguarded the secrets of Ascension from potential misuse.

Our culture, guided by stories and enforced by religious belief, further prevents us from realizing our potential and metamorphosing—*morphing*—into the higher beings we were created to be. We identify with our fallen state rather than our ascended state. We tell ourselves this story repeatedly. In fact, this version of reality has been told so many times, it is practically written in concrete in our minds.

The spiritual dilemma this cultural conditioning engendered reminds me of the story of the two caterpillars chatting on a log. A beautiful butterfly gently floats by. One caterpillar says to the other: "You'll never get me up in one of those butterfly things."

That is our essential predicament. We don't believe we can morph, or we are afraid of morphing, or afraid of what people might think if we do. Therefore, we don't.

However, beginning with the Sumerians, the Egyptians, and the Hindus—and running through Judaism and Christianity—the sacred and mystical art of alchemical transformation, regeneration, and ultimately of resurrection and Ascension *while alive* has run parallel to the traditional religious teachings that have tried to stamp it out.

The way through this soul dilemma is to create new stories that open the imagination to our true potential. We must flip the script from the negative, "You'll never get me up in one of these things" to the inspired, "How do I learn to fly?"

AFTER THE FALL: THE RISING

Adapa's story is the Sumerian version of the creation and fall of humanity. It is the basis for the later story of Adam and Eve as told in the Book of Genesis. Creation stories, particularly Genesis in the Christian Holy Bible, tell us humans were made in the image of God. This belief is foundational to Judaism, Christianity, and Islam, which makes it the operating principle of billions of people. We know this story. We accept it, whether it is true or not. But how many give enough thought to what this description actually means?

In Genesis, God said, "Let us (Elohim) make mankind in our image, in our likeness, so that they may rule over the fish in the sea and the birds in the sky, over the livestock and all the wild animals, and over all the creatures that move along the ground." (Genesis 1:26-27).

Notice that this verse states that Elohim made humans in his image. Elohim is a plural noun and is translated as "gods," "divine beings." The best understanding of Elohim seems to be the "strong one(s)" or the "mighty one(s)." They are reported as being radiant, similar to the Anunnaki.

In chapter three of Genesis, Adam and Eve are expelled from Eden after being warned away from the wisdom of the serpent, who is equated with Enki. After Eve received this wisdom, the first humans were expelled from Eden, "lest humans become like God."

The precise meaning of the "image of God" (*imago Dei* in Latin), and what it means to become *like God*, has been debated for centuries in the church. Do we resemble God because we share DNA? Is the God of the Old Testament a physical being? Did God "come down," incarnate, and take flesh-and-blood human form in order to make us? Are we made from a mold? Can we break it?

The answer to all these questions is *yes/no*. Although God is Spirit (John 4:24) and does not have a body like a man, when he appeared visibly to men, according to the Old Testament record, he did so in the form of a human body as an Elohim or god—with a lower-case "g."

We are not talking about God, the creator of the universe. We are talking about little gods with massive superpowers. This observation is fundamental to opening our ascension path.

Philo, writing in Alexandria in the first century, knew the very name *Israel* meant "the ones who see God." If this *theophany* (a visible manifestation of God) was in human form, appearing as a human being who walks and talks and cares and acts, this means there is something about the human body that is uniquely appropriate to God's manifestation of himself. He must have designed the human body, and coded our DNA, with this in mind. Otherwise, why wouldn't God appear as an orb of light or some other form?

Wait. God *did* appear in light form. A humanoid one. More than just having a humanoid appearance, we learn God's body (or the god's body) is luminous and rainbow-like.

Ezekiel wrote, "The appearance of the brilliant light all around Him was like that of a rainbow in a cloud on a rainy day. This was the appearance of the likeness of the glory of the Lord. And when I saw it, I fell facedown and heard a voice speaking" (Ezekiel 1:28).

What we must remember is that, as the Zohar—the chief book of the Jewish Kabbalah—says, "When Adam dwelt in Eden, he was clothed in the celestial garment, which is the garment of heavenly light … light of that light which was used in the garden of Eden." (Zohar II.229B)

This means that, when humans lived in Eden, we were in a different form. We had "perfect" bodies of light—like the gods—which were symbolized by a robe of rainbow light. Our soul lived in a high realm or plane of consciousness. We were surrounded by pure light and pure love, at one with all that is.

Then, as the book of Genesis says, we ate the fruit and our souls fell into physical manifestation or the matrix of Maia/Gaia. We left our robe of light behind and began to experience reality through the ego, our lower nature.

Yahweh punished us by giving us garments of skin…human skin. We realized we were "naked" and "imperfect." Both of these terms mean we were no longer in our original light bodies or wearing our robes of light, but rather, were now in human bodies.

Unfortunately, knowledge, or remembrance, of our true selves was lost when we were exiled from Eden. After Eve partook of the forbidden wisdom of the serpent, she and Adam were expelled from Eden.

> As Genesis 3:21 tells us: 21 "And the Lord God made garments of skin for Adam and his wife, and He clothed them. 22 Then the Lord God said, Behold, the man has become like one of Us, knowing good and evil. And now, lest he reach out his hand and take also from the tree of life, and eat, and live forever…"

The garments of skin covered our original light bodies.

> Genesis 3:24 continues the story: "So the Lord God sent him out from the garden of Eden, to work the ground from which he was taken. 24 So He drove the man out. And He placed cherubim east of the garden of Eden with a sword of

fire that turned every way. They kept watch over the path to the tree of life."

In this version of the story, we were warned not to seek the ascension teachings that enable us to return to our Source. Once again, we are dealing with priests standing between us and the Divine.

OUR ESSENTIAL COSMIC PREDICAMENT

According to Judeo-Christian tradition, our exile from Eden is the singular event in human history. It is the motivating incident in Western Civilization, which is based on Jewish, Christian, and Islamic beliefs sourced from the Sumerians. When Adam and Eve partook of the fruit in the Garden of Eden, and fell, a transformation took place. Their world changed. Their bodies changed. Mortality began. We are still living this story. We are still seeking to return to Eden.

Western civilization is based on the Judeo-Christian premise that the actions of Adam and Eve, the first humans, are responsible for (y)our current spiritual malaise. One day, we will reverse this fall. Eden will be restored, and we will rise.

Even if you don't believe Adam and Eve existed, their archetypal story is still a guiding narrative of our times. Civilization began with Eden and ends with the return of Christ and our ascension to, or unification with, a celestial realm known as the Kingdom of Heaven. It does not matter what name you give to this realm; the destination is the same. This reunification completely transforms Earth and introduces a time when all live with righteous values and, hence, have expanded spiritual capabilities. The era is marked by a new heaven, a new Earth, and a new human.

This story explains our essential cosmic predicament. We are hybrid beings who have been denied immortality and the motivation to ascend. However, enfolded within these stories is the promise that we *can* ascend. We have the ability. We are genetically wired to ascend.

The desire to ascend is an answer to an ancient call to transform our world, our planet, into a place of righteousness. You know this world exists. You might also realize this transformation is your mission.

THE POSITIVE FALL

There could be a positive intention behind our engineered "fall." I say "engineered" because *Atra-Hasis* says Enki planned for us to end up in this condition. A return to the acorn analogy explains why.

Acorns contain the seeds that can grow new oak trees. The only way new oak trees grow is if acorns leave their source, the tree, and fall to the ground. This is part of the tree's lifecycle. It is how they reproduce. Falling acorns are like the sperm of the tree. When they reach the ground, they impregnate the earth and can grow new offspring or be carried off to new locations by wildlife.

The seed is a perfect metaphor for the soul and its Ascension. So is sperm. The seed or incarnating human soul emerges / falls from the spiritual realm and plants itself in the earthly body of clay (or DNA) for the production of earthly fruit. That is why it is said, "by our fruits that we are known." A perfect version of our self is enfolded within this seed. A similar theory of sperm containing a miniature but complete version of the person, the homunculus, completes the seed-sperm connection.

The worry is that the soul / seed, while planted on Earth, might be allowed to rot or wither. Just as the body needs food and water, so does the soul. It craves wisdom, especially about the meaning of its existence. This is why seeds are the *basis* of knowledge and wisdom. This shows up in the language we use to describe transformation. People seek to turn over a new leaf or nip things in the bud. We go out on a limb to seek knowledge.

For me, the propagation of life is the real reason the Anunnaki came to Earth. They weren't here on a search for gold. Their mission was about souls. Specifically, it was about how souls can be lifted from the Earth and ascend to their source. The Anunnaki were gardeners. They came to Earth to spread life. The first thing humans did for them was to tend their gardens. At first glance, this seems like a lowly job. But when you think about it, who wouldn't trade their earthly life for an opportunity to tend the garden of the gods in the heavenly realm?

Seeds, as tiny and humble as they are, are a beautiful and powerful sacred metaphor for life, consciousness, and the Ascension of your soul. The gardening metaphor runs through many Ascension stories. As we go, I encourage you to think of the human soul, your soul, as the seed in the acorn that turns its body into an oak. Like the acorn, the blueprint or code for the oak is written within your soul. My goal is to guide you to seeing the oak.

THE RAINBOW LIGHT BODY

In Tibetan tradition, the body (tangible matter) is composed of five elements: earth, air, fire, water, and space-time. Through meditation, adepts can perform a mind-over-matter "dissolution" or "evolution" of the body into a five-colored rainbow light, leaving behind only hair and the toe and fingernails, which have no nerves to be transmuted. The "new," transformed body is called the Rainbow Light Body.

One of the primary Tibetan teachers is Padmasambhava. Tibetan paintings, called *thangkas*, portray Padmasambhva on a lotus throne. His body is surrounded by rainbow light that emanates from his heart center.

In his hand, he holds the vajra, the symbol of compassion in action. He has dissolved his body into light and can now deliver compassion in an expanded way.

Accounts of humans achieving this transformation go back thousands of years. Through a process called *jalu powa chemo* a complete transference of the consciousness into the rainbow body takes place and one enters the immortal state. This transformation is the highest human achievement. The Tibetans refer to it as the "Great Perfection."

Once the adept attains the Rainbow Body, it is possible to travel to any of the other twelve star systems where this teaching is taught. According to the tradition, this knowledge is known to advanced civilizations beyond our planet who have been watching over us for millennia.

PERFECTION

The word "perfect" means to be whole, holy, complete, righteous, and compassionate. All of these words are synonymous with Ascension. As in the Great Perfection or Rainbow Body tradition, in the ancient Egyptian ascension teachings, the human body is considered an intermediate phase, a transitional state, or a bridge. Enlightened and compassionate souls can "quicken" or dissolve the body into its pure essence and bridge the worlds.

Ascension and light body manifestation is linked with this transmutation, transformation, or perfection. This conversion is, in fact, a *distillation* process, similar to the way muddy water turns into invisible vapor after a day of hot sun. The puddle no longer exists, but the atoms that once made it continue on in another phase or form. In the Rainbow Light Body practice, one is able to phase between these states of being. The reason one would do so is to be able to share compassion with a greater number of people.

In my journeys I have used the word "perfect" like a golden needle to thread my way through and between the world's religious and spiritual traditions. From Sumeria to Iran to Iraq to Egypt to India to Tibet to Southern France, I have woven threads of the secrets of our original, pure or perfect light bodies into a many-colored coat or garment worn by the risen beings who are our instructors in this ascension.

These traditions say that this perfect light self, referred to as a "garment of light," is within us, awaiting unveiling. We can become a traveling sensation if we reveal it. We all have been spending lifetime after lifetime working on this realization. Our learning is cumulative. We carry it with us.

The Tibetans teach that we must first be introduced to our true nature. Next, we must visualize this experience, and then we can live it. The light body and ascension can be attained in one lifetime, say the Tibetans. It may even be this lifetime. Some of us believe we can do this, while others don't.

Most every sacred tradition has a term for this garment and a technology for its attainment, along with histories of opposition to their quest for perfection and descriptions of a continuum of heavenly beings who came to teach about and demonstrate its manifestation.

There is an exact parallel between the Tibetan depictions of the perfected ones and Christian images of the resurrected Jesus. It is possible that Jesus learned the secrets of the Great Perfection while living in India and/or Tibet during his so-called "lost" or "missing" years between the ages of twelve and thirty. I believe it is the same as the *melammu*.

It is key for us to understand that Jesus was referred to as the "Second Adam" because his mission was to undo the "fall" of Adam and Eve. He came to show us the way to ascend.

THE ROBE OF LIGHT

In order to enter the heavenly realms, say numerous, ancient, spiritual traditions, we must be dressed appropriately… lightly, that is, in a sacred robe of radiant splendor. Attaining this robe or light is our life's purpose.

The soul travels to and from the ascended realm in an ethereal-type body, sheath, or envelope that Iamblichus called the "soul-vehicle." This is already within us. The sheath is an intermediary between the physical body and the immaterial soul. During the descent of the soul to Earth, this sheath acquired impurities from the cosmic gods and realms it passed through.

In order to ascend, the sheath must be cleansed and purified. Higher spiritual beings can help the soul. As the soul-vehicle reaches higher levels of purification, it becomes illuminated by a process called *photagogia*, or "evoking the light" which fills the soul with Divine illumination. According to one early ascension keeper, Iamblichus, this process "illuminates with Divine light the ethereal and luminous vehicle of the soul."

Ascension, or attainment of our original light body, is symbolized by a white robe. Every spiritual tradition has a name for our "super" ascended body. In Sufism, it is called "the most sacred body" and "supracelestial body." Taoists call it "the diamond body," and those who have attained it are called "the immortals" and "the cloudwalkers." Yogic schools and Tantrics call it "the Divine body." In Kris yoga, it is called "the body of bliss." In Vedanta, it is called "the superconductive body." In the alchemical tradition, the Emerald Tablet calls it "the golden body." The Tibetans call it the "Rainbow Light Body," while Christianity refers to it as the "glory body" or "born-again body."

These terms are descriptive and informative of our next state of being, the accelerated and ascended state. In many traditions, this garment was considered transmittable, indicating that it is quite likely a teaching rather than an actual, physical garment.

For example, in the story of Elijah's ascension, we learn that, as he was being translated into his light body form and transported to heaven via a celestial chariot, he transmitted his robe of righteousness to his priest, Elisha.

On Earth, this robe, or the teaching it symbolized, enabled Elijah to perform miracles. His acquisition of this glorious body and luminous garment signals transition from an earthly being to a celestial being. To enter the heavenly realms, we must be dressed appropriately.

Later, when Elijah reincarnated as John the Baptist, he re-attained the robe of light and transferred it to Jesus at the baptism. Jesus demonstrated what I call "the light body effect" at his Transfiguration, when he morphed into light.

TURNING INSIDE OUT

The robe of light may not be something that we acquire or recover, as much as it is something we uncover or "unturn" from within. It is already present within us. It is woven of light, but its luminosity is covered over by false perceptions about who we are and by our identification with our flesh-and-blood bodies rather than our light bodies.

For Buddhists, the ultimate goal of spiritual practice is to awaken to one's own true nature, which is the nature of a fully enlightened Buddha. The Rainbow Light Body is primordially present and enfolded within us. To "make" it, we tune into it and unfold it.

Turning into light is actually a "turning inside-out" of what is hidden within our lives. In our ascension, our outer more closely matches our inner. As Saying 22 of the *Gospel of Thomas* vividly states, matching the inner and the outer is the key to entering the Kingdom of God.

"Jesus said to them: When you make the two one, and when you make the inside as the outside, and the outside as the inside, and the upper as the lower, and when you make the male and the female into a single one, so that the male is not male and the female not female, and when you make eyes in place of an eye, and a hand in place of a hand, and a foot in place of a foot, an image in place of an image, then shall you enter [the kingdom]."

The Essenes, the tribe of primarily Jewish mystics out of which John the Baptist, Mary Magdalene, and likely, Jesus, emerged, were great scholars, researchers, and practitioners of the most advanced spiritual teachings on Earth. They said their teachings on perfection came from the angels. This teaching matches the Tibetan light body teaching, which they said came from the stars, meaning it is a universal teaching. It is my hope that my linking the Essene Perfect Way, the Tibetan Great Perfection, and the Christian Born-Again traditions is received today in the spirit of love and unity with which the Essenes received it 2,000 years ago.

Then, as now, the promise is the same. When we live from our light bodies, we become a new being, a born-again being in the here-and-now. We live a life like those of the seraphim, the Essenes, and Christ. Filled with the supernatural power of the Holy Spirit, we are able to do the same things they could do.

In the next chapter I will present a timeline of ascension teachings from ancient to modern times. It will come as no surprise to see how many times the concept of the robe, the rainbow, and the Rainbow Light Body are referenced.

OUR ASCENSION TIMELINE

———— ❧❧ ————

*T*he modern quest for ascension should include a study of the history of ascension literature and the practitioners who walked this way long before us and cleared our path, often at great personal sacrifice. It is not too bold to say that all contemporary statements and beliefs about Ascension are rooted in the ancient ideas expressed by the masters we will be discussing.

While there are many valid contemporary viewpoints on Ascension, I turn to the ancient ascension keepers for these matters. This is not to discount the modern mystics or channelers who are advancing our awareness and understanding of this process. The new words we use today may be different from the ancient ones—for example, the *5D realm* versus *Kingdom of Heaven*—but the meaning and origins of the concepts are the same. It is vital to understand the seed, the roots, the trunk, and the tree.

We are clearly experiencing the fruit of seeds planted long ago. To understand this fruit and the trees upon which it grows, we must get to know the gardeners who planted the trees, and whose garden we tend.

The timeline that follows is not just a literary timeline; it is a sequence of events that have led to our present ascension moment. It would take volumes to tell the stories of all who have laid the golden bricks in our path of souls or who have put rungs on our ladder to heaven. What follows is a bird's-eye look at the major steps, especially those from Buddhist and the western traditions of Judaism, Christianity, and Islam.

Along the way, we will seek and spotlight the actions and practices they employed for their ascension.

Let us begin with the ancient Egyptians.

OUT OF EGYPT

The oldest religious texts in the world are the ancient Egyptian *Pyramid Texts.* Dated to c. 2400 B.C., they were written in hieroglyphs carved on the walls of the subterranean tomb of a pharaoh named Unas, located beneath a pyramid at Saqqara, Egypt. These texts are a collection of spells and utterances meant to protect and sustain the pharaoh during his afterlife journey and enable his spiritual transformation or transfiguration into an *Akh.* The Akh is portrayed as a glorious being of light who, effectively, has the same personality as he did on Earth, but is freed from the body and now sits among the gods. Some believe the Akh body was earned by successive lives as a good person.

According to the *Pyramid Texts,* during a time called *Zep Tepi*—the First Time or the Golden Age—civilization was established by intermediaries between the gods and men called the *Urshu,* a category of lesser divinities whose title meant "the Watchers." The Urshu lived on the Earth as the guardians and guides of mankind. The great British Egyptologist, E. A. Wallis Budge, refers to them as "angels."

The ancient Egyptians viewed their civilization as a legacy coming directly from these Divine celestial beings, who existed in Egypt thousands of years before the pharaonic dynasties that were established in 3100 B.C. It was they who established the first ascension schools on Earth. For thousands of years, the mystery schools of Egypt sustained the secret wisdom and knowledge of these ancient ascension masters. This knowledge was protected by being kept hidden and secret, and only revealed to initiates by a master.

The *Pyramid Texts* were intended as a guidebook for the ascension of the pharaoh's Akh through the various stages of the afterlife journey. This journey included the resurrection of the Akh and its finding its rightful place among the gods and the stars. The ancient Egyptians believed that, without these texts, the pharaoh would not be able to ascend.

The texts established the profound belief that death was not the end of one's soul. Instead, death was seen as a step taken or a tool used by the soul to transition into another way of living. Interestingly, the *Pyramid Texts* describe the king ascending upon a throne. This motif of the flying ascension throne is common in many later ascension texts. Also, the soul is portrayed flying like a bird to higher realms.

These texts are the first written account of a celestial ascent. It is no coincidence that this first text is an ascension text, or that it was found near a stepped pyramid referred to as the "Stairway to Heaven." As we will elaborate, Ascension was the singular pre-occupation of the ancient mystics and adepts. They planted the seed of the ascension tree upon which we feed.

I need to emphasize that these texts, and the extraordinary teachings they contain, were initially kept secret. Common people were not privy to these teachings, which were reserved for the elite initiates and priests. Scholars did not hear about them until they were discovered by French Egyptologist, Gustave Master in the early 1880s.

It is utterly remarkable that these secrets were preserved for all those thousands of years. From 2500 B.C. until the time of Moses (1300 B.C.), Pythagoras (600 B.C.), and Jesus, and continuing until the end of the Roman Empire (A.D. 400), initiates continuously made pilgrimages to Saqqara to learn ascension secrets.

A particular theme that originated in the *Pyramid Texts* is that of passing through gates into other realms. Specifically, there were seven gates. These later became associated with halls or holes in space through which the ascending soul travels. The ancient Egyptians considered it essential to know the names of the guardians of these gates, and/or the necessary passwords.

The *Pyramid Texts* introduced another core ascension concept or practice: the pure soul, or purifying the soul. To the ancient Egyptians, the object of Earth life was to pass the "weighing of the heart" test when, at Judgment Day, the heart was weighed against the feather of cosmic truth, righteousness, and balance, called the "maat." If the heart was pure, it would balance with the feather. If not, the soul would be recycled until it attained purity.

Maat is a state of perfection to which all nature is called and for which everything strives. The quest for *maat* was at the center of the ancient Egyptian civilization. The pharaohs led by it. Individuals were expected to "do maat" in their everyday affairs. They felt that human beings should conduct their lives in a righteous manner so their hearts would weigh favorably on the scale of justice. Those who had lived righteous lives would be judged as able to move on or ascend to higher levels of existence.

Testing or judgment is not a one-off experience. In spiritual affairs, our heart is constantly on the scale.

The importance of purity of heart as a pre-requisite for Ascension was emphasized 1,500 years later in the Psalms of the biblical King David: "Who shall ascend the Mountain of the Lord?" the priests would ask. "Who shall stand in this Holy Place?"

The answer was clear and unequivocal: "Those who have clean hands and pure hearts" (Psalm 24:3-4).

Another core ascension tenet introduced by the ancient Egyptians was that ordinary people can ascend. This was demonstrated by the evolution of the Egyptian mummification rites, which emerged from Saqqara.

At first, only the pharaohs—who were considered incarnations of the gods—were afforded these elaborate rites and magical, spiritual procedures. Over time, the rites would be performed on wealthy individuals. As the process gradually became more affordable, even average people were mummified—and so were their pets, especially cats. This development demonstrates that the idea of the immortality of the soul and its ability to ascend to higher regions was known and accepted as a possibility for more than just the elite priests.

THE STAIRWAY TO HEAVEN

The *Pyramid Texts* can be thought of as a code for the soul's ascension. It is no coincidence that they were discovered near the stepped pyramid at Saqqara. This pyramid was built for King Djoser in c. 2600 B.C. and is said to be the oldest man-made stone structure on Earth. Its purpose was to facilitate the king's journey to rebirth in the afterlife, which is why it was known as the "Stairway to Heaven." The great Giza pyramid, which Egyptologists claim was constructed soon after the Saqqara stairway, was known as a transmutation machine and a place of Ascension.

Many similar step pyramids have since been constructed throughout the world, including in Babylon, Cambodia, and the Americas. These pyramids are extraordinary structures where the gods came down to meet, and sometimes mate with, humans. They were also repositories for the ascension knowledge bequeathed by the gods.

Imhotep built Djoser's pyramid at Saqqara. An architect, master stone builder, magician, scientist, and medicine man, Imhotep was the first historical person to be deified. In the process, he became the first historical figure to ascend.

Imhotep's name means "he who comes in peace." He was known as a son of Ptah, the god whom the ancient Egyptians said came from the star Sirius and fashioned the human body.

Interestingly, Ptah's hieroglyph includes a string that resembles a double helix of DNA, as well as a compass and a square, the tools of transformation. He was known as the god of Egyptian stonemasons, craftsmen, scribes, and priests. He created technologies like a resurrection stick and the Ark of the Millions of Years, the ship upon which the throne of the pharaoh sailed across the waters of eternity. Imhotep wears a feathered cloak.

Imhotep's eminent position in Egyptian society is documented on the statue base of Djoser, which is now kept in the Egyptian Museum in Cairo. That base contains the most important and only known titles of Imhotep: "prince, royal seal-bearer of the king of Lower Egypt, high priest of Heliopolis, director of sculptors." Given the extraordinary privilege of being named on a royal statue, it is supposed that Imhotep was, in fact, considered a respected member of the king's family. Some even think he was Ptah incarnated.

In the millennia after this transition, Imhotep's influence grew. He was deified during the New Kingdom and a worship center and ascension school emerged at Saqqara. As noted, this center was in continuous operation for more than 2,000 years. By Roman times, Imhotep had acquired god-like status. The Greeks identified him as their god of medicine, Asclepius.

Archaeologists and Egyptologists fervently seek Imhotep's lost tomb, certain it will contain immense secrets, and likely even lost knowledge about Ascension.

PTAH AND IMHOTEP'S ASCENSION PRACTICES

These foundational ascension teachings, practices, or insights that were derived from Ptah and Imhotep should be spotlighted:

First, Ptah is an Egyptian creator god who conceived the world in his mind and manifested it through the power of his spoken word. He spoke and the world came into existence.

The ancient Egyptians believed the Divine operated through everything and that everything was Divine, including themselves. The Middle Kingdom *Coffin Texts* affirm that "my soul is God. I am the creator of the Word." This means our world—and everything in it, including you—are Divine manifestations that originated in the mind of Ptah or in a higher mental plane. Ptah's thoughts became real on Earth once he spoke them into existence. In essence, he made our world out of thin air.

This concept raises many more questions about the nature of our reality than can be addressed here. The key take-away is that our world emerged from a higher plane. This is the realm from which we descended and the place to which we seek to ascend, for rebirth.

The word spoken by Ptah is a vibration. The ancient Egyptians had profound knowledge of the science by which sound or vibration influences matter. This concept is found in the Gospel of John 1:1, which says: "In the beginning was the Word, and the Word was with God and the Word was God." God is the vibration that descended into materiality and is in everything. This metaphysics is found in the earlier Book of Genesis (1:2-3), which says: "And the Spirt of God was hovering over the face of the waters. Then God said, Let there be light and there was light."

A 22nd dynasty hymn to Ptah said he crafted the world in the design of his heart. The Shabaka Stone, from the 25th dynasty, says Ptah "gave life to all the gods and their *ka*s as well, through this heart and this tongue." This suggests the power of Ptah's spoken word rippled out into creation as an outward manifestation from his heart.

This tells us of the power of a unified heart and mind. Ptah conceived the world in his mind, felt (or nurtured) it in his heart, and manifested it with his speech. The heart is the bridge between realms.

We, too, have the power to craft our lives by mirroring Ptah in a sacred way. The heart-mind connection he demonstrated is the path to wholeness and holiness, because understanding this link connects us with the Divine realm "above" our world.

As with other avatars, Ptah possessed the ability to instantly manifest his thoughts. He had the ability to empower his imagination with a finished vision, put his heart into it, and materialize a finished product. Today, we call this *heart-brain coherence*, which is considered a miracle healing modality. At a minimum, the skill of attaining heart-brain coherence turns us into self-healers. Fully maximized, this state is the key to self-glorification or attainment of the Rainbow Light Body.

The power of God, the Divine energy, is in the heart. We connect with this power through our intention to be of Divine service.

Next, we feel the emotion of the finished or completed work. For instance, imagine yourself as a glorified light being. As in the example of the acorn and the oak, a different, ascended, you already exists within you. Now, supercharge this vision with the emotion from your heart and speak it into manifestation by saying, out loud, your name. As you speak your name, attach to this vibration a vision and a feeling of your whole, holy, complete, and perfected self.

You can speak holy words, holy sounds, and words of power of your choice as you feel this intention. According to this tradition, "heka" was the word that God uttered to release the Divine energy that brought the world into manifestation. Speaking this word brought the invisible into the visible.

Then, we speak this vision into manifestation. An example of this is the practice of repeating positive affirmations. An affirmation is a positive statement, usually beginning with the words "I am" that is said aloud with the intention of uniting your conscious and subconscious mind. For example, "I am light." When we repeat these words over and over again, they change our thoughts, our actions, our bodies, and our destiny. With this tool, we can command what is in our imagination to become manifested in the visible world and let our voices ring into the Divine mind field.

A second ascension insight and practice comes from Imhotep's title as *director of sculptors*. A *sculptor*, from the Latin "to carve," is an artist who shapes clay, stone, marble, wood, and other materials into two or three-dimensional art. The finished creation is carved into walls or other surfaces or erected as a free-standing statue. There is much metaphysical contemplation to be spotlighted here.

Foremost is the claim that the first humans were molded from clay. From Sumeria to Egypt to Palestine to Europe to South America, holy books and legends tell us humanity was made from clay or dust. In Genesis 2:7 we read: "And the Lord God formed man [of] the dust of the ground, and breathed into his nostrils the breath of life; and man became a living soul." Isaiah 64:8 says: "But now, O Lord, you are our Father; we are the clay, and you are our potter; we are all the work of your hand." This earthen substance can be interpreted as a metaphor for DNA. As our bodies rise from within the DNA clay, we become like sculptures.

If life as a free-standing being is your choice, then you are on the ascension path. As this metaphysical view evolved during the next few centuries, writers like Plotinus, in the Enneads, describes working on one's own inner statue and inducing the presence of God in your art.

I shall return to this theme of the art of Ascension in a later chapter. For now, we honor Ptah for providing fundamental ascension practices that have been used for millennia.

STARGATE BABYLON

We can find parallels between the step pyramid or Stairway to Heaven of Saqqara and the Sumerian, Akkadian, and Babylonian ziggurats. A key example is the Etemenanki of Babylon or the Temple of the Foundation of Heaven and Earth. It is here that our timeline winds.

This temple is thought to be the biblical Tower of Babel (Genesis 11:4-5). The word "babel" means "gate to God." According to Genesis, the builders of this tower wanted to make a name for themselves by creating a mighty city and erecting a tower with its top in the heavens.

"And the Lord came down to see the city and the tower which the children of men built. And the Lord said, "Behold, the people are one and they have all one language, and this they begin to do; and now nothing will be impossible which they have imagined to do. Come, let us go down, and there confound their language, that they may not understand one another's speech." So the Lord scattered them abroad from thence upon the face of all the Earth; and they left off building the city." (Genesis 11:6-7)

God (or a god) disrupted the work by so confusing the language of the workers that they could no longer understand one another.

The tower of Babel was clearly intended as a conduit to heaven. However, God did not want company or for humanity to do the impossible. Our tower was smashed and our hopes for Ascension dashed.

Structures like this tower were thought of as portals or stargates. Specific knowledge of codes and software were required to make them work. Making a name for oneself involved an ascension to a higher level of existence. The making of the tower and the making of the name went together.

Now, the word *name* here refers to a vibration, but it also is equated with renown. When we make a name for ourselves, it means we have achieved a higher level of distinction than others. Renown also means fame and glory. Those who have it have luster, a glow, and stardom. They shine. Now, this is interesting, as the word *glory* refers to luminescence. God radiates glory.

Is it possible that the builders of the Tower of Babel were making Rainbow Light Bodies in preparation for journeying through the stargate?

ENMEDURANKI AND THE ASCENSION TABLETS

We are told that the Tower of Babel was constructed during the third generation after the great flood by Noah's great-grandson, Nimrod (Genesis 10-11). Interestingly, he was called "mighty one" due to his possession of the *melammu* cloak of the gods.

Following the flood, all of humanity was destroyed except the family of Noah, and presumably, all the world's knowledge was also destroyed. If this is true, it raises an intriguing question: Where, exactly, did the builders acquire the knowledge to build "a ladder that reached into heaven" along with knowledge of how to scale this ladder?

The answer is, it must have been brought over from the time before the flood. Nimrod must have inherited this wisdom from Noah, who, by the way, was called "perfect in his generation." Now, you might have always thought Noah survived the flood by building a wooden ark. No one has ever suggested this "ark" was like the Ark of the Millions of Years of ancient Egypt or that, as a perfect one, Noah crafted his light body. However, this is where the evidence has led me.

The Tower of Babel was constructed in the land of Shinar, present-day Iraq. Turning to ancient Sumeria, we find the story of an intriguing ascension seeker named Enmeduranki, whose story is dated to c. 2900 B.C. but who is claimed to have lived before the great flood. His name means "chief of the powers of the Dur-an-ki" or "the meeting-place of heaven and Earth." The Sumerian King List claims he ruled for 21,000 years!

Scholars have determined that he is the prototype for the Biblical figure of Enoch. The Book of Genesis says Enoch "walked with God" and was the first human to ascend; Enoch was no more because God took him away (Genesis 5:18– 24). Noah was Enoch's great-grandson. As noted, he too, walked with God. To me, this means Noah also ascended.

Enmeduranki was the king of Sippar, a city noted as a wisdom center and the only city to survive the biblical flood. After the flood, the survivors went to Sippar to dig up the writings of the antediluvian sages. In the texts, Enmeduranki is taken to heaven by the sun god, Shamash, and Adad, the Rainmaker. He was then given a golden throne, indicating a metamorphosis into one of the gods and membership in their Divine assembly.

Enmeduranki knew the secrets of the gods and, as a consequence, he was transformed. He now had access to the higher mysteries of the gods. He transmitted this information to his son.

A tablet from Nineveh, dated to 1100 B.C. and published by Wilfred Lambert, tells that, while in heaven, Enmeduranki/ Enoch also was given the "tablets of the gods," the bag with the mystery (secret) of heaven and Earth, oil on water, and the cedar staff. For a human, a meeting with a heavenly being and acquisition of the heavenly tablets or heavenly secrets is the ultimate experience. Enmeduranki's acquisition of these ascension tablets indicates he arrived at the gate of the gods. He gained access to the mysteries of the gods, the Divine knowledge, and the insight to understand the hidden meanings ordinarily concealed from normal humans. He was now an ascended and translated man. He even had a large, golden throne.

After his translation or transformation, Enmeduranki became one of the Holy Ones —called "Watchers"—who sit on a golden throne alongside the gods. He is assigned guardianship of the Divine mysteries. The Nineveh tablet tells us he acquired new celestial titles, including learned savant, a diviner, a priest, and a guardian of secrets. Enmeduranki was also given a new job.

He greets those who ascend to heaven, guides them, and reveals the celestial secrets to them. He is a mediator or bridge between heaven and Earth, a psychopomp, and the first "next human."

Something profound happened with the writing of this tale. From Enmeduranki's story we learn that a human being *can* cross the boundary between the material realm of humans and the transcendent, immaterial realm of the gods. A human can make an ascent to heaven, see the celestial realms, enter the chamber of the gods, and experience the presence of God. He can then be transformed into an "angel" through that experience, return to Earth to tell everyone about it, and inspire them to believe that they, too, can take this ultimate journey.

AMENHOTEP, SON OF HAPU

Fast forward on our timeline to 1250 B.C., West Bank, Luxor, Egypt. Another descendant of Ptah was Amenhotep, son of Hapu, a 13th century B.C. scribe, astronomer, mathematician, and designer of the Karnak temples built under Amenhotep III. He is responsible for constructing one of the wonders of ancient Egypt, the so-called Colossi of Memnon. These two massive stone statues of Amenhotep III were constructed as guardians of the king's mortuary temple in front of the Valley of the Kings. Weighing 720 tons each, the statues reach a massive sixty feet and represent Amenhotep, Son of Hapu's, highly advanced knowledge of engineering and mastery of stone works.

When Strobo, the Greek writer, visited the West Bank in 20 B.C., he recorded that every morning when the first rays of the sun bathed one of the statues, it inexplicably let out an audible singing note.

Like Imhotep, Amenhotep, son of Hapu, is well-known to scholars as a human who reached beyond human heights during his life and was remembered hundreds of years after leaving the Earth.

Scholars have studied the idea that Amenhotep attained *apotheosis* or human transformation into a Divine being. Like Enmeduranki, he then became an intermediary between the god Amun and humans. This is a role that was shared by Enoch after his apotheosis and transformation into the archangel Metatron.

The examples of Imhotep and Amenhotep are proof that the Egyptians believed that human ascension, and its resultant divination, was not merely a metaphorical matter of ceremony but could transpire in metaphysical actuality. These men were not pharaohs, but rather were common men of learning and wisdom. Though separated from one another in life by 1,200 years, that were unified in their activities as Sons of Ptah and keepers of the secrets of ascension.

Both Imhotep and Amenhotep, son of Hapu, ascended through the heavens to become divinized. They were real people whose existence is attested to in many monuments and documents. However, in time, they were revered as gods and worshiped in their own temples. They are examples of human beings who, by their use of the therapeutic wisdom, were held up as examples to be equaled by their fellow mortals.

How they attained apotheosis is at the heart of our odyssey.

The healing chapel at the Deir el-Bahari temple of Hatshepsut was dedicated to Amenhotep, son of Hapu. An *ostracon* (a writing on a piece of pottery) by a man named Polyaratos tells us that dream incubation was practiced at Deir el-Bahari. The writing contains a narrative describing one worshiper's miraculous recovery from a long-suffering disease after a visitation by Amenhotep in a dream. The long-dead Egyptian, he wrote, "stood beside" the man and healed him.

This provides us with another important tool for ascension: lucid dreaming and dream incubation. Both practices are aimed at connecting with higher realms—and the beings who dwell there—for the direct or specific purpose of healing.

A common example of dream incubation today is the practice of focusing on a personal problem prior to sleep with the intention of inciting a dream that will help solve the problem. More esoteric examples involve the use of pre-sleep rituals such as meditating on symbols or images to shape the content of subsequent dreams. Historical texts tell us that deities would appear in dreams and deliver messages, knowledge, and healing. Even more fantastically, some believed the dreams opened a portal through which the deities could travel between worlds.

The earliest practice of dream incubation is found at Saqqara. It is safe to say it is another gift of Ptah.

MOSES

In what is perhaps the most well-known, but mystifying, stories of the Bible, Moses ascended Mount Sinai sometime during the 14th to 13th century B.C. and had a Divine encounter with Yahweh, which was the name for the God of the Israelites. Yahweh gave him heavenly tablets.

Yahweh normally dwelled in the celestial Sion, the heavenly Jerusalem and city of the living God (Hebrews 12:22). When Yahweh manifested on Earth (Exodus 25-31), he first did so in a burning bush, a shrub covered in flames but mysteriously not consumed by the fire. There, he gave Moses two sets of tablets and instructed him to build a specially constructed tabernacle and then a temple. Both structures were built in accordance with a heavenly plan as the "house" or "footstool" of God. These were to be precise copies of heavenly originals. Moses also was told to place the Ark of the Covenant in the tabernacle and then the temple.

After Moses returned from the mountain, his face was shining with the glory of God (Exodus 34:29). The Israelites were so terrified, or possibly awed, by this that Moses began wearing a veil over his face to shroud the glory (Exodus 33-35).

The Lord spoke to Moses inside the tabernacle from the Ark of the Covenant. A cloud, the *glory* of the Lord, filled the place. He used to sit on the *kaporet* "atonement piece" or "mercy seat" (Exodus 25:17), a covering made of pure gold which rested upon the Ark. Two golden cherubim with massive, fifteen-foot wings, had been placed on either end of the mercy seat, facing each other, forming an enclosure. Yahweh's presence would manifest between the two cherubim (or Seraphim) and speak from the *cloud* over the oracle (Leviticus 16:2). God was believed literally to be present. When he left, he exited the same way he came.

Obviously, the repetition of the throne symbolism catches our attention. It is perhaps *the* ascension symbol and suggests that Moses' encounter with the burning bush was about Ascension.

A sensational text featuring the theme of Yahweh as a human-type figure on the throne is the mystical drama known as *Exagoge*. Written by Ezekiel the Tragedian, this text is only known by fragments of the original recorded by the Christian historian Eusebius. The original play is thought to have been written in the second century B.C. and is, thus, the oldest piece of Jewish drama available. It is exemplary of the Jewish mysticism widely circulating at the time.

In this drama, during a vision on Mount Sinai, Moses sees a noble being sitting on a throne wearing a crown and holding a scepter. The being beckons Moses to him and hands him the scepter. He tells him to sit on the throne and gives him the crown.

Moses assembles this "kit." The noble man disappears. Suddenly, Moses sees the whole Earth around and stars beneath his feet. He is in the stars and is treated to a cosmic tour! Moses has beamed from Sinai to the stars via the Ark-throne.

Another text describing an ascent via the throne and the acquisition of illumination is found in the 3rd-4th century Gnostic book, *Odes of Solomon*, which begins: "I went up into the light of truth as if not a chariot (throne); and the truth took me and led me" (Ode 38).

This throne is the Ark of the Covenant, or more properly, God's Ark-Throne. It might seem strange to think of the Ark of the Covenant as a throne and an ascension portal or "stargate device," but if 21st century terminology is applied, that is exactly what the descriptions of the ark in use suggests.

MOSES SHINED

We are not told for how long Moses radiated light. The apostle Paul (2 Corinthians 3:13) claimed the light faded and Moses continued to wear the veil to prevent the Israelites from seeing this. The veil was designed to make people think his face was still shining, even though it wasn't.

Significantly, Paul also said that because Moses beheld the glory of God, his face reflected God's glory. Henceforth, New Testament believers think that by beholding the glory of God, we are transformed into that glory. As I noted earlier, glory is symbolized by a rainbow. If we substitute the word "glory" for "Rainbow Light Body," a new light radiates from this story.

Paul says that seeing Christ is the answer for how we behold this glory: "And we all, who with unveiled faces contemplate the Lord's glory, are being transformed into his image with ever-increasing glory, which comes from the Lord, who is the Spirit" (2 Corinthians 3:18).

Paul does not comment on why the glory would have faded from Moses, prompting him to hide behind the veil, but we may hypothesize that he stopped doing some of the things that got him there.

KING DAVID AND SOLOMON

In *c.* 850 B.C., King David had the Ark of the Covenant brought to Sion by the Levites (1 Samuel 7:1,2; 1 Chronicles 13:7), while he himself, "girded with a linen *ephod*" (the holy garment), "danced before the Lord with all his might" and in the sight of all the public gathered in Jerusalem.

According to 1 Kings 6:1, Solomon dedicated his temple 480 years after the Exodus began. Since the date of Solomon's Temple dedication has been fixed as 961 B.C., we then have a proposed date of 1441 B.C. for the Exodus of Moses and his encounter with the burning bush.

When Solomon's Temple was constructed as the Ark's permanent home, a veil was hung before the Ark that separated the "holy place from the most holy place" (Exodus 26:31-33) or Holy of Holies (which we will explore in detail later). Following the "on Earth as in heaven" (as above, so below) adage, the Holy of Holies *is* "heaven on Earth." In this sacred space, the Lord was literally present.

There are some fascinating legends about the construction of Solomon's Temple, including that it was not made with human hands. Solomon, himself, is also the subject of many legends, including those that say he was a great magi and that he ascended to the heavens upon his throne. This tale became the basis for the legend of his famous magic carpet.

There are various descriptions of Solomon's temple in the Old Testament, the most detailed being in Kings and in Chronicles, but people usually turn to the account in 1 Kings to learn about the structure's purpose and appearance.

The veil dividing the Temple into two areas was covered with stars. A short staircase or ramp led from the outer part of the temple (the Holy Place) to a slightly elevated, special inner room that housed the Ark (the Most Holy Place or Holy of Holies) (1 Kings 6:19).

The Holy of Holies is described as a wooden cube measuring twenty cubits (thirty ft.) on each side (1 Kings 6:20; Ezekiel 41:3-4). The room surrounding it was thirty cubits (forty-five feet) high (1 Kings 6:2). Its walls were covered with pure gold (2 Chronicles 3.8).

Spectacular reliefs decorated the golden walls of the inner and outer rooms of Solomon's Temple, including bas reliefs and engravings of cherubim, palm trees, and flower patterns (1 Kings 6:29). Solomon built his temple as a garden to represent the garden of God, perhaps even the Garden of Eden. In practice, it was a portal to Eden.

At the dedication of the temple, the Ark was moved therein (1 Kings 8:6-9).

1 Kings 6-8 tells us the golden cube of Solomon's Temple also housed a sacred symbol or device referred to as the *Ashram*, a pillar or pole sacred to the goddess *Asherah* and her temple priestesses, who were called *prostitutes*. The word translated "cult prostitutes" in 2 Kings 23:7 (*q'deshim*) has the same consonants as "holy ones"(*q'doshim*) or angels.

In many English translations, "Asherah" is translated as "sacred tree." Proverbs 3:18 tells us of female wisdom: "She shall be a tree of life to all who lay hold on her."

THE DIVINE FEMININE ASCENSION WISDOM

In 1967, Raphael Patai was the first historian to mention that the ancient Israelites worshiped both Yahweh *and* Asherah. In *The Hebrew Goddess*, he calculated that "the statue of Asherah was present in the temple for no less than 236 years, two-thirds of the time the Solomonic temple stood in Jerusalem." This worship, he asserts, was part of the legitimate religion, approved and led by the king, the court, and the priesthood. Scholar William Dever and other archeologists who studied goddesses claim Hathor is Asherah.

Patai calls her *Hathor-Asherah*. On an Egyptian plaque, she is listed as Qudshu, Hathor-Asherah, Anat, and Astarte. They are all the same goddess. Qudshu is the Egyptian form of the word Qetesh, Qadesh, Kadesh, or Qadeshet. It means "(feminine) Holy One" or "holiness" in Hebrew, Canaanite, and Egyptian.

In Mesopotamia, she was called Inanna. Her priestesses were the holy ones at Solomon's Temple.

1 Enoch tells how the Jews worshipped the Queen of Heaven. Images portray her as an angelic figure with wings.

The most notable feature of the stories of all these goddesses is the concept of Ascension. It is fair to say that Ascension is the business of the Queen(s) of Heaven.

What this means is that there was another wisdom tradition practiced in Jerusalem and the Temple of Solomon. This other wisdom was about Ascension, and it included the Divine Feminine.

It is tantalizing to think of this group of mystics, under the guidance of angels, who were practicing Ascension. What happened to them? Why did this practice not take hold for the masses?

The reason is given in 2 Kings 23:7, where we learn that King Josiah, who reigned from 641-609 B.C., "pulled down the house of the sacred prostitutes (*qdsym*) which was in the Temple of Yahweh and where the women wove curtains for Asherah." Josiah removed the Asherah from the holy place.

As the book of Chronicles tells us, in 623 B.C., during the eighteenth year of his reign, Josiah began refurbishing the Temple of Solomon, which the previous kings had neglected. During the restoration, a high priest named Hilkiah discovered a book, "the book of the law," that had been given to Moses. When Josiah discovered what it said, he summoned all the subjects of Jerusalem and Judah to the temple and read for them the new law. This completely changed the history of the world and became a pivotal moment in our ascension timeline.

The new law book is called the Book of Deuteronomy, or the *book of the covenant* (2 Kings 23.2). It was said to have been received by Moses in the burning bush. At its heart are the Ten Commandments, the laws of Yahweh.

Deuteronomy's laws and ordinances were upheld as the new wisdom and understanding. This was completely different from the older, Ascension-based, Divine Feminine-delivered, wisdom tradition, which was now forbidden by Josiah.

We can begin to understand this older Divine Feminine ascension wisdom tradition by following Josiah's actions. The discovery of Deuteronomy compelled Josiah to go on a rampage, destroying the shrines and high places of worship, the Asherah and her images. He removed their name from the land. He purged the temple of the symbols of the Divine Feminine.

Deuteronomy forbade alien religions, altars, pillars, ashrams, and images. All were to be destroyed, smashed, and burned (Deuteronomy 7:5, 12:3, 16:21). Worshipping celestial beings, the host of heaven, became a capital offense. Looking at the stars was also forbidden, for fear the people would, once again, worship the host of heaven. All forms of divination were outlawed (Deuteronomy 18.9-14). Punishment for disobedience was death by stoning (Deuteronomy 17.2-5).

God got a divorce. Ascension wisdom was banned.

Despite trying to eradicate it, the priests could only suppress the original quest for transformation and Ascension. It was too widespread. Instead, they took the position that these mystics who claimed to have ascended did not "really" ascend. They merely had hallucinatory or visionary psychedelic experiences that they believed were real.

From this moment forward, we see the appearance in literature of priests who say things like "You can only ascend when you are dead" or "Those who claim to ascend don't really do so" or "No one actually turns to light."

This, clearly, was a changing of the gods and a closing of the gate to heaven. If Solomon's Temple was an ascension center, it was now officially locked and unloaded of its key symbols, especially those of the goddess.

EZEKIEL AND THE MERKABA

In 586 B.C., Nebuchadnezzar and the Babylonians conquered Jerusalem, flattened its walls, and stripped Solomon's Temple of all its treasure. Then they set the city ablaze and returned home to Babylon with the treasure of the temple and a group of royal prisoners-of-war.

The Greek 3rd Book of Ezra (1 Esdras) tells us that the Babylonians: "took all the holy vessels of the Lord, both great and small, and the ark of God, and the king's treasures, and carried them away into Babylon" (1 Esdras 1:54). Thousands of Jews also were exiled to Babylon.

This exile is often thought of as a mass deportation. In reality, the Babylonians were precise in their selection of which citizens they transplanted. Among the exiles of this "Babylonian captivity" were the elites and upper classes of Jerusalem.

Included in the intelligentsia were the prophets Daniel and Ezekiel, to whom every conscious ascender owes a debt of gratitude. When they arrived in Babylon, it was a fully functioning Ascension mystery school.

We are told in the book of the Holy Bible that bears his name that Ezekiel was near the banks of the river Chuber in Babylon on July 28, 593 B.C. when suddenly, a whirlwind—a great cloud with brightness about it—appeared. Inside this cloud were four living creatures. Ezekiel saw wheels within wheels that had the ability to fly. Above them was a throne, and on the throne was the likeness of a man. Ezekiel describes the being on the throne as "something that seemed like human form" surrounded by a rainbow (Ezekiel 1:26). Ezekiel then saw this chariot/throne leaving the Temple of Solomon. First a cloud filled the inner court of the temple, and then he realized that this was the brightness of the glory of the Lord (Ezekiel 10.3-4).

A throne/chariot of god who is a humanoid being surrounded by a rainbow?

This vision, which is the core of the Book of Ezekiel, became the focal point of another key ascension teaching: Merkabah mysticism. Merkabah (*Mer-kavah*) (also *Merkaba*) means "throne-chariot" or "sacred boat" and refers to the craft in Ezekiel's vision. *Khav* or *Khab* is the *cab* (car) of God. The Merkabah mystics claimed to be able to duplicate Ezekiel's experience of ascending to the heavens in this chariot, or sailing the stars in this boat. In addition to Ezekiel, these Jewish mystics favored Enoch as a way-shower.

The Merkaba mystics established a practice that is still valuable to us today. They visualized themselves ascending through the seven heavens and through seven halls or palaces to the Throne of God. As they ascended, they encountered various angels and gatekeepers. By uttering the correct, secret name of these angels, they were able to pass through to the next hall.

Merkaba mysticism tells how angels and righteous ones initiated humans in the secrets of heaven. Many of the fundamental teachings of these mystics, who followed the ascension mysticism of the Jews, can be traced directly to the *Pyramid Texts*. For example, a core concept of Merkaba mysticism is the provision of secret seals or sigils that permit the initiated to ascend.

Nothing is said in the Bible about the Ark of the Covenant after the Jews returned from Babylon. There is also no mention of God having a female counterpart. Deuteronomy mentions none of these items because they were associated with the original wisdom tradition of the Divine Feminine. Nothing is said about Ascension after this, either.

Just imagine if, suddenly, all you believed about higher consciousness, Ascension, and your potential as a spiritual being was ripped away from you and forbidden by the decree of a king or president. Imagine that you were then exiled to a foreign land and told that you could never again see your home.

The Greek researcher Herodotus probably didn't visit Babylon, but his writings in the 5th century B.C. book *Histories* provide astounding details about one of the city's step pyramids, the Etemenanki, including the temple rituals and its purpose.

According to Herodotus, the Anunnaki god Marduk, a celestial being, would manifest as a human in this temple and meet with a human priestess atop its peak, where a sacred marriage would take place. Other times, the king would ascend to the top of the ziggurat and mate with the goddess Inanna (Ishtar).

According to Algis Uzdavinys, writing in his fascinating work, *Ascent to Heaven in Islamic and Jewish Mysticism,* the ziggurat is a "cosmic pole" a "ladder" or a "mountain" that leads to Heaven where the gods Marduk, Shamash, Adad, and others dwell at the throne of the supreme Anunnaki god, Anu.

Interestingly, Uzdavinys says the seven-tiered ziggurat represents *the rainbow of covenant.* The seven tiers correspond to the seven rays: red, orange, yellow, green, blue, indigo, and violet.

In this way, the ziggurat/tower can be imagined as a rainbow stairway or conduit to the Divine realm.

This description, the *rainbow of the covenant,* links with the rainbow glory of God motif and gives support to my theory that the Tower of Babel story of humanity seeking to "make a name" for itself is about the Rainbow Light Body.

Marduk had a second temple in Babylon, the *Esagila* ("the lofty house"). Also called "the house that lifts its head high," the Esagila was his place of Ascension. Marduk built this temple to establish communications between the Earth and the cosmic realms. Importantly, the Esagila is presumed to be a prototype for the Temple of Solomon in Jerusalem.

At the turn of the 20th century, German archaeologists found many small objects inside the temple. Of special interest was an oblong piece of lapis lazuli on which the image Marduk had been carved with great skill. Marduk in the image was clothed in a star-covered cloak and held in his left hand a ring and staff, which were his symbols as the sun god.

The star cloak. The *melammu.* The garment of glory. The robe of light. The Rainbow Light Body.

BUDDHA

Speaking of star cloaks, another wearer of such a garment was a young prince named Gautama of the Shakyamuni clan. From his home in India, this man taught a mixture of ascension ideas also found in shamanic, Sumerian, Egyptian, Judean, Babylonian, and Vedic beliefs. His followers believed he was a historical human who possessed supernatural spiritual powers and who ascended to a pure land called *Parinirvana,* where he watched over them.

The location of his ascension was Mount Sri Pada in Sri Lanka, also known as Adam's Peak; a giant footstep crushed into the ground can still be seen there today. Believers say it is a footstep Buddha took during his Ascension. Others say it is the first footstep Adam took after being cast out of Eden.

Siddhartha Gautama, the Buddha, was born c. 563 B.C. The fall of Babylon, and the return of the exiles to Jerusalem, took place while he was a young man. The merchants of India must have heard about this and spread the news around Asia. The first settlement of Jews in India was established in Cochin in southern India in 562 B.C., a year after the birth of Buddha. Could this colony have met Buddha and shared Solomon's wisdom with him? The possibility is fascinating to contemplate.

In 534, at the age of twenty-nine, Siddhartha Gautama abandoned his family and wealthy life, an act called the "Great Renunciation." Within a few years, he spent seven weeks sitting under a bodhi tree and became the Buddha, the Awakened One. Gautama, from then on, was known as "The Perfectly Self-Awakened One," the Samyaksambuddha—one who has achieved a state of perfect enlightenment.

Based on the premise that mystical insight and illumination can only be attained by direct, Divine intervention or contemplation and reflection (just like the Essene *Book of Mysteries* says), Buddha taught the *Eight-Fold Path* as the means to attain our goal of spiritual enlightenment.

TWO STREAMS

During the two centuries after Buddha's transition, the religion that took his name, Buddhism, split into two schools or streams: *Theravada* and *Mahayana*. These are known as the great and small chariots or vehicles of enlightenment. Remember, Merkabah means "throne chariot."

Theravada (thera "elders" + vada "doctrine") is "The Doctrine of the Elders" or "the Way of the Elders." This school of Buddhism follows the original teachings of Buddha, which are known as the Pali cannon. Followers strive to become *arhats*, or "perfected saints" who have attained enlightenment, shining bodies, and Nirvana.

Mahayana Buddhism—also known as the "Great Vehicle"—developed the idea that enlightenment can be achieved in one lifetime—and even by the lay person, not just by the monks and nuns. Mahayana Buddhists hope to become not *arhats* but *boddhisatvas*, saints who have become enlightened but who unselfishly delay Nirvana to help others also attain it, as the Buddha did.

This form of worship often includes veneration of celestial beings and other Buddhas and *boddhisatvas*; ceremonies, religious rituals, and magical rites; and the use of icons, images, and other sacred objects and symbols, including the Buddha's footprints.

Paramita ("perfection" or "completeness") is a Pali term for the qualities that must be fulfilled by a *bodhisattva* during the course of their spiritual development. Interestingly, the Sanskrit word *paramita* means "from beyond," "gone to the beyond," or to cross over to the other shore. It is derived from "para" and "ita" meaning "across, over, or beyond." This term suggests the idea of an ascension portal as the way to go beyond to other, supernatural realms (Nirvana).

Paramita may also be translated "perfect realization" or reaching beyond limitation. In other words, it refers to the achievement of a transcendent state, which, I believe, can be equated with the concept of angels.

Buddhists believe six qualities lead to realization: generosity, discipline, patience, joyful endeavor, meditative concentration, and wisdom awareness. Through the practice of these six paramitas, we cross over the sea of suffering (samsara) to the shore of happiness and awakening (Nirvana); we cross over from ignorance and delusion to enlightenment. Each of the six paramitas is an enlightened quality of the heart, a glorious virtue or attribute—an innate seed of perfect realization within us. The paramitas are the very essence of our true nature. Practicing them today is as fruitful as it was 2,300 years ago.

Clearly, an ascension acceleration was taking place in ancient Babylon and India. The next 600 years would see a proliferation of ascension texts, but also brutal efforts to suppress these teachings.

PYTHAGORAS

The influence of the Greek philosopher Pythagoras (570 to 495 B.C.) is woven throughout the philosophy of western civilization. As an initiate of the Egyptian mystery schools, he traveled extensively in Egypt and India and was mixing with the Babylonian sages within decades of Ezekiel and Daniel. After traveling, Pythagoras returned to Greece and taught the transmigration of souls and the belief that our souls originated from a Supreme Being.

Like the Buddhists, Pythagoras sought redemption from the cycle of earthly rebirths. He viewed the soul as trapped or imprisoned in the body as punishment. In *Admonitions Concerning Embodiment of the Soul, Banished to the Earth*, Empedocles (c. 500-430 B.C.), who echoed the teachings of Pythagoras, spoke of the "alien garment of the body." Only through a process of purification could the soul return to its source.

The Pythagoreans were divided in their schools into *novices* and *perfect* (there is that word again). They separated themselves from other humans, lived in monasteries, practiced vegetarianism, greeted the rising sun, shared property communally, and wore white garments. Many of the key Buddhist/Pythagorean philosophies and practices were later mixed into the foundations of the Essene lifestyle. Some even claim Pythagoras was an Essene or Therapeutae (another group of pre-Essene Essenes). It is difficult to say with certainty that Pythagoras was an Essene. It is more easily proven that the Essenes were Pythagoreans.

Pythagoras taught that each species of creatures had what he termed a "seal," given to it by God, and that the physical form of each was the impression of this seal upon the "wax" of physical substance. Thus, each material body was stamped with the seal of its Divinely given pattern. Pythagoras believed that ultimately, man would reach a state where he would cast off his gross nature and function in a body of spiritualized ether, which would be in juxtaposition to his physical form at all times, and which might be the eighth sphere, or Antichthon. From this space, man would ascend into the realm of the immortals, where, by Divine birthright, he belonged.

Pythagoras also taught that all the stars are inhabited. The further into the galaxy one traveled, the higher and lighter the beings who lived there.

PLATO'S ACADEMY

The foremost disciple of Pythagoras was Plato. His academy, formed in Athens in c. 438 B.C. was an ascension school that operated for more than 100 years and was the source of much of modern ascension teaching.

It was Plato who gave the world the conception of forms or ideas. For him, the unseen world was the real world. In it there were laid up the forms, the ideas, the perfect archetypes and patterns of which everything in this world is a pale and imperfect copy.

In his *Allegory of the Cave,* Plato said the world of senses that we live in is not the "real" world. In simplest terms, there is, in the unseen world, a perfect idea of a chair of which all man-made chairs are imperfect copies. This world of space and time is not the real world, and the things we can see and touch are not the real things. The real world is the invisible world beyond. This perfect world can only be accessed via contemplation and intellect.

Second, Plato taught the ancient idea of the astral body, the subtle body intermediate between the soul and the mental body. This is the body in which the soul journeys to the stars.

The word astral means "of the stars." It is the same as the glory body, radiant body, celestial body, and light body.

Plato taught that the stars were composed of an ethereal element or quintessence that differed from the four earthly elements—and the human psyche was composed of the same material.

Plato saw the Divine in everything. He considered the world one living thing. The goal of his students was to participate in creation. Later students, like Iamblichus, read the works of Pythagoras and Plato with the belief that doing so could deify the soul. Neoplatonists posited that we have two bodies: the body of light, which is the immortal vehicle of the soul, and the body of breath, which is the mortal vehicle. They developed practices, called *theurgy,* aimed at turning themselves into gods.

Theurgic practices were meant to cleanse the light body, to restore contact between our earthly and Divine selves. For Plato's lineage of mystics, the soul's vehicle or subtle body is traditionally divided into two kinds, which merge into each other as the vehicle becomes increasingly purified of material elements. These two vehicles are the etheric or spirt body and the celestial or luminous one. According to Plato's teacher, Aristotle (384-322 B.C.), the light body is of a rarer, finer quintessence, moving in a circular fashion and taking the image of the physical body when it descends.

Along the way, we weave an *ochêma*, a spherical body, like those of the gods, that is part material and part spiritual. Purifying this sphere has been compared to the purification of the subtle body in yoga. This is done through diet, physical exercise, chanting, burning incense, prayer, and most powerfully, visualizations. In these practices, the imagination, which was considered to be a part of the light body, played a substantial role. The 5th century Platonist Hierocles describes the discipline as follows:

"We must take care of the purity relating to our luminous body, which the Oracles call 'the light vehicle of the soul.' Such purity extends to our food, our drink, and to the entire regimen of our mortal body in which the luminous body resides, as it breathes life into the inanimate body and maintains its harmony."

A key takeaway here is to think about all that we eat from the perspective of the light body. Is the food we consume nourishing to our luminous body? Is there a light body diet?

When the *ochêma* is sufficiently purified, theurgists may perform *photogogia*, the technique of filling the porous *ochêma* with light. Iamblichus describes the process as follows:

"Photogogia illuminates with divine light the ethereal and luminous vehicle of the souls, from which divine visions take possession of our imaginative power moved by the will of the gods."

This illumination was the theurgist's goal. I am convinced it is another manifestation of the Tibetan Great Perfection or Rainbow Light Body teaching.

200 B.C. TO A.D. 400

After the Babylonian captivity, especially during the three centuries before Jesus, the belief that the boundary between humanity and the Divine is "permeable" became widespread in the Mediterranean world. Until that time, there was a perceived (and enforced) boundary between heaven and Earth that was uncrossable by human souls, unless invited. This meant only a few souls ascended.

One secret of boundary crossing was that by reciting the stories of the visionary ascents of past ascenders, one could repeat the visionary ascent of those people. Simply reading about the Ascension is powerful. However, this is more than a thought experiment. As one thinks about it, and visualizes or replicates Ascension, one begins to live their Ascension in advance. Thinking about our Ascension builds anticipation. It concretizes it in our minds. To me, this suggests that these texts are coded to tap the mythic imagination.

From 100 B.C. to A.D. 1000, Jewish Merkabah mystics or mystics of the Throne Chariot or *sacred boat* took the ancient ascension stories and repeated them. In these texts, humans are encouraged to rehearse or visualize journeys to heaven and an experience with the glory of God. The chariot is a useful visualization. The soul is described as the charioteer, whose mastery of the two horses—which are the passions and appetites of the soul—enables the soul to ascend into the heavens. Self-control is a hallmark of the awakened soul.

In their visions, these mystics would enter the celestial realms and journey through the seven stages of mystical ascent: the seven heavens, seven halls, or seven throne rooms.

The key to a successful journey is acquisition and reciting of the secret name(s) of God. One of these secret names, for example, was used by Moses to part the Red Sea. The ultimate goal of the ascent is to not only see God's face, but also to become an angel and join the celestial tribe of angels.

Part One

After their return from exile in Babylon in 538 B.C., the Jews rebuilt the Temple of Solomon, but it was incomplete. The Ark of the Covenant and all its components, including symbols of the Divine Feminine and Ascension, were missing. Also absent was the Shekinah or Divine Presence. The Second Temple of Solomon was deemed nonfunctional for some. For others, it was deemed totally fake.

In reaction, a group of righteous Jews, called Essenes, did something very clever. They created a community in which they, themselves, became the pillars of the rebuilt temple. Each of them became high priests, putting on the crown and robe and ascending on the throne. According to their community rule, they were calling in a high celestial being.

The Essenes are Jewish mystics who, extraordinarily, claimed to be living with angels who taught them how to transform their human flesh — in a flash — into the celestial flesh of the angels. Radiant, luminous, and shining, this flesh is composed of a rarefied "perfect" spiritual substance that is as real or "solid" in the higher realms as our physical body is on the Earth.

The angels the Essenes were living with, who taught them the art and science of *angelification* or human transformation into angels, were called the Watchers, the mighty *Seraphim*, the *"winged and fiery serpents"* and *"burning ones."* Their swirling bodies are composed of pure love and light and are full of eyes, an appropriate attribute of those who watch or guard God's throne. In Christian art, the Seraphim are sometimes portrayed as six-winged and covered with feathers.

In the Jewish mystical book, *Hekalot Zutarti*, we learn, "their walking is like the appearance of a lightning bolt; a vision of them is like a vision of a rainbow; their faces are like a vision of a bride; their wings are like the radiance of the clouds of glory."

According to the ancient accounts of our fellow travelers, these extraordinary lightning-like beings have supernatural powers, including shape-shifting and phasing between the immaterial and material realms.

— 68 —

Attainment of this "light body" is the next step in human spiritual evolution.

According to the Dead Sea Scrolls, the Essenes alienated themselves from the rest of society to "perfect" themselves in order to prepare and make way for the visitation of a high celestial being and to lead a revolution in human evolution by transforming themselves into angels and the Earth into a planet of righteousness.

The scrolls reveal the Essenes were also obsessed with transforming themselves to be like their visiting angels and their state of being (in light bodies), so they could ascend to and enter a celestial city called Sion or the New Jerusalem. In Hebrews 12:22, we learn this place is inhabited by "angels gathered in joyful assembly and just humans made perfect." The Essenes sought to take their place at this family gathering of angels and perfect ones.

My research leads me to believe that the Essenes living in Jerusalem and Alexandria, Egypt c. 150 B.C. to A.D. 66 were practicing Buddhist Rainbow Light Body techniques referred to as the Great Perfection.

The high celestial being they were "calling in" was Jesus.

JESUS

In Christianity, Jesus provides the solution to our soul dilemma. In his incarnation, he showed the way for humanity to undo the Fall. When most think of Ascension, they might think of the ascension of Christ to heaven. Forty days after the crucifixion, according to the Bible's reports, he rose bodily into the heavens in front of witnesses who were both human and angelic. Scripture says he now dwells in a transformed body that is a radiant or glorified light body in a heavenly place or Divine dimension. Christians view this pivotal event in human history as the end of one era of human history and the beginning of another. This "new era" would see the emergence of a new, special human, a "whole," "holy," and "perfected" one with expanded spiritual capabilities such as healing, compassion, and Ascension, as exemplified by Christ. The era also would include a "new Earth" where righteousness (spiritual alignment) is the basis for human life.

Significantly, in some Christian art, when Christ is shown ascending, he does so in a sphere, similar to the one Plato taught about.

For the mystically minded, Christ's Ascension is seen as a momentous step forward in a long mission or timeline led by advanced spiritual beings who manifested planet-wide over thousands of years. They came to uplift humanity to attain this higher or ascended state of being. Jesus represented this advanced race and demonstrated the way all of us can attain our own Ascension. As Jesus taught, "these things that I do you will do greater" (John 14:12). He called us to perfection as the way to follow him to the celestial realms: "If thou wilt be perfect, go and sell that thou hast, and give to the poor, and thou shalt have treasure in heaven: and come and follow me" (Matthew 19:21). This call is in perfect resonance with the Tibetan perfection teaching.

Jesus further declared that the secret of Ascension was in two commandments. The first is to "Love the Lord your God with all your heart and with all your soul and with all your mind" (Matthew 22:37). The second is equally important: "Love your neighbor as yourself. No other commandment is greater than these" (Mark 12:30-31). These simple commandments replaced the ten commandments of Moses.

Christ's Ascension is an event and a state of being attainable by all who seek eternal life, according to the Holy Bible. It is a call, a promise, that some will attain this higher level and live with the angels from now on, separate from the rest of humanity. A more hopeful interpretation is that all of humanity will attain this ascended state of existence.

In some early Christian art, Jesus ascends in a rainbow sphere held aloft by the ophanim wheels of the angels. These are the same as Ezekiel's wheels. As I wrote in *The Secret of Sion*, the Ascension is a fantastic subject in Christian art, as well as a theme in mystical writings. By the 6th century, the iconography of the Ascension had been established; by the 9th century, Ascension scenes were being depicted on domes of churches. The *oculus* or eye of the dome is considered the Gateway of the Sun. From this gateway at the top of the dome rises the World Axis, the link between heaven and Earth. Domes, therefore, are the threshold or gateway of the spiritual world. Thus, portraying Jesus ascending in/through a dome symbolizes him traveling through the wormhole.

The Syriac Rabbula Gospels (c. 586) include some of the earliest images of the Ascension and feature what would become standard Ascension iconography. They offer the first illustration of Jesus ascending in a radiating or glowing, almond-shaped ring or *mandorla* ("gate") lifted to heaven on a chariot composed of whirling wheels within wheels and many-eyed angels' wings. A *mandorla* is the liminal, threshold space where two circles overlap. It is a powerful symbol of the psychological and spiritual realm where opposites merge, planes or dimensions of existence meet, and transformation occurs.

The whirling wheels within wheels motif is comparable to Ezekiel's vision, as are the lion, bull, man, and eagle, which are symbols of the four evangelists Matthew, Mark, Luke, and John and the four creatures that guard the Throne of God.

This early gospel set the blue tone for all future Christian ascension images. However, I believe the imagery originates with the images of the pharaoh on the wormhole boat at Denderah. While the Egyptian art shows a side view of the ascending figure, Christian art shows the same concept from the face on. In Egypt, we see a side view of the wormhole.

In Christian art we are looking down its throat as Jesus travels through it. The blue sphere is to be imagined as a portal or gateway. I wondered if this is what Plato meant by the light body being a sphere.

In Jewish mysticism this ascension sphere is called the *merkaba* or "throne chariot." This is derived from Theravada (Great Chariot) and

Mahayana (Little Chariot) Buddhism, as well as Zoroastrian and Egyptian feathered-throne mysticism.

Where do Christians who ascend go? Hebrews 12:22-24 answers that question. It tells of a heavenly place called Sion or New Jerusalem, where angels are "gathered in joyful assembly, along with just humans made perfect." In Christian art, the enthroned Christ is surrounded by a rainbow.

MOTHER MARY

Historically, Mother Mary is believed to be the first Christian to attain perfection and to ascend. While it is not recorded in the New Testament, the Assumption of Mary is one of the Marian dogmas and mysteries of the Catholic Church. The English word "assumption" is from the Latin *assumptio* meaning "taking up." At the moment of Mary's death, according to the story, Jesus Christ himself descended and carried her soul into heaven.

On November 1, 1950, Pope Pius XII defined the Assumption of Mary to be a dogma of faith: "We pronounce, declare, and define it to be a Divinely revealed dogma that the immaculate Mother of God, the ever Virgin Mary, having completed the course of her earthly life, was assumed body and soul to heavenly glory."

She completed her earthly life. She ascended into her body of heavenly glory or possibly her Rainbow Light Body.

One tradition states that Mary lived out her life in Ephesus, modern-day Turkey, where she prepared for her Ascension. All of the disciples had fled Jerusalem after the crucifixion, resurrection, and Ascension of Jesus. They were all called back to Jerusalem for Mary's Ascension.

According to Catholic tradition, Mary was living in the house of the Apostle John, in Jerusalem, when the Archangel Gabriel revealed to her that her death would occur three days later. The apostles, scattered throughout the world, are said to have been miraculously transported to be at her side when she died. The sole exception was Thomas, who had been delayed. He is said to have arrived three days after her death in a cloud above her tomb and to have seen her body leaving, bound for heaven.

He asked her "Where are you going, O Holy One?"

Mary took off her girdle and gave it to him and said, "Receive this, my friend"—and then she disappeared.

Later, Thomas was taken to his fellow apostles and asked to see her grave so that he could bid her goodbye. Mary had been buried in Gethsemane, according to her request. When they arrived at the grave, her body was gone, leaving only a sweet fragrance.

Within Catholicism there is a debate concerning the Ascension. Was it an *assumption* or a *dormition*? In the assumption, she rose from the dead after a short period and then ascended to heaven. In the dormition, she was "assumed" bodily into heaven while still alive.

This debate pre-dates Catholicism. Beginning with the Sumerians, the Egyptians, and the Hindus—and found through Judaism and Christianity— the sacred and mystical art of transformation, regeneration, and ultimately of resurrection *while alive* has run parallel to traditional religious teaching, which has tried to stamp it out. Even today, religious teachers will tell you Ascension is only possible once you are dead.

Mary's assumption further connects with ancient ascension practices we have already discussed, notably lucid dreaming. The dormition is known as the "sleep of Mary." Could Mary have been using ancient, lucid dreaming techniques?

Mary was regarded as a "second Eve" whose purity restored her to the paradise from which Eve had been driven. She was considered the perfect example of our union with God. Christians believe that Jesus is the "second Adam," who came to show us the way to our original perfection and light bodies.

Like Jesus, the Virgin Mary is considered an ascended being who is capable of phasing or appearing in our light spectrum as an apparition. An apparition is looked upon as a resurrection. The first Marian apparition occurred in A.D. 40 when Mary appeared to Saint James the Apostle, the brother of Saint John the Evangelist, on the bank of the river Ebro in Saragossa, Spain and asked him to build a church dedicated to her, promising that "it will stand from that moment until the end of time in order that God may work miracles and wonders through my intercession for all those who place themselves under my patronage."

As hundreds of sightings on several continents attest, Mary attained a light body capable of being seen by hundreds of thousands of people. Mary Magdalene, Christ's chief apostle, also ascended. Their lineage continues to this day with millions of people actively doing the spiritual work—including yoga, meditation, chanting, and visualization—that will raise them to a higher level of spiritual awareness and existence.

A.D. 70

The Second Temple of Solomon was completely destroyed by the Romans in A.D. 70. The artificial platform upon which it was built remained. This site is still hugely important to millions of Jews, Christians, and Muslims.

After the destruction of the temple, the Essenes and other Jewish mystics fled to Syria, Turkey, France, England, and India, among other places. Knowledge of these Jewish mystical ascension practices went with them.

In the next several hundred years, the apocalypses emerged. These ancient Jewish visionary writings describe how their protagonists ascended to the heavenly realms and received revelations from celestial beings. This is the meaning of the word *apocalypse*. In the second century A.D., in this text, the prophet Isaiah rises through seven levels of heaven. At each level, he transforms until he reaches the throne of God.

The setting is the time of Hezekiah, the king of Judah and great-grandfather of Josiah. Isaiah is invited to the king's court from his home in Gilgal, where giants had constructed a stone circle. Forty prophets and sons of prophets had made the journey to Jerusalem to greet him and to be healed by his hands laid upon them. While Isaiah was speaking, the Holy Spirit came upon him. Suddenly, he became still, and his consciousness was taken from him. His eyes were open, but his mouth was closed. An angel from the seventh heaven appeared and provided for him a vision of the celestial world, hidden from all flesh, and then took him on a journey through seven heavens.

The fact that Isaiah's eyes were wide open indicates a visionary or even hallucinatory experience. A similar report of an Ascension while in trance is found in *The Acts of Thomas*. It describes the experience this way: The "twin" of Jesus, the apostle Thomas—whose mission was in India—anoints parts of his head and body with oils, places a crown on his head, stares at the ground with a branch of reed in his hand, starts chanting, and then transforms.

When Isaiah reached the seventh heaven, he saw the heavenly company: "And there I saw Enoch, and all who were with him, stripped of their robes of the flesh, and I saw them in their robes of above, and they were like the angels who stand there in great glory" (Isaiah 9:8-9).

These ascensions are clearly intended to be interpreted as visionary only. They are mind movies or ascension simulations. Like Isaiah and Thomas, John the Revelator (Revelation 4:2-11) ascended to heaven. He saw a door open in heaven. There, he saw one seated upon a throne that shone like a rainbow. Twenty-four elders clad in white robes gathered around the throne, as did throngs of angels. Lightning flashed from it. In front of the throne was a sea of glass.

This is the holy city of God, said John.

In Gnosticism, the purpose of life is to find the way for the Divine Spark to be released from the human form and return to God and the Divine Realm or Land of Light. Christ is seen as an avatar of the Light who has taken human form to lead humanity back to the light. This idea is expressed most eloquently in the opening lines of the Gospel of John.

John 1:1 "In the beginning was the Word was with God, and the Word was God."

Then, in John 1:14: "The Word became flesh and made His dwelling among us."

Jesus calls the higher state of ascended consciousness *the Tree of Life.*

"To him that overcometh will I give to eat of the Tree of Life, which is in the midst of the paradise of God" (Rev. 2:7).

I believe that what is overcome is the lower egoic/flesh nature.

All human growth and development is aimed at returning humanity to this pure state of being, our original state of perfection and existence in our light bodies.

In short, in the esoteric traditions, humans must remember that we originally were beings of light. Ever since the Fall we have sought the means to escape or transcend the confines of our biological bodies and return to our original light bodies.

MOHAMMED

In A.D. 610, a man came to Jerusalem and the Temple Mount from Mecca in Saudi Arabia on a pilgrimage. His name was Mohammed. The story of how he came to Jerusalem is one of most extraordinary in all ascension lore. History knows Mohammed as the founder of Islam. According to Islamic belief, he was God's final prophet and messenger.

Destiny found Mohammed when he was thirty-five years old, when he was involved with a well-known story about setting a black stone in the wall of the Kaaba in 605 C.E.

The Kaaba, or *The Cube*, is a cuboid-shaped stone building at the center of the pilgrimage site in Mecca, Saudi Arabia. It is the most sacred site in Islam. Five times a day, Muslims pray by turning to the east, towards Mecca and the sacred stone in the Kaaba.

In Islam it is believed the Kaaba is situated directly under a house in the seventh heaven. Angels descended directly over the site and paved the foundation with stone.

It was there that Adam was sent after the expulsion from Eden. It is believed the gateway extends from the Kaaba to heaven directly, making it an extreme energy or Ascension point.

The Qur'an states that Abraham and his son Ishmael constructed the Kaaba, after Ishmael had settled in Arabia. A passage in the *Apocalypse of Abraham* states Abraham was shown the stars. An angel came and took him on a journey, during which Abraham went into a trance. His spirit left his body and the angel took him to watch a star in the process of transformation. When he came back, he entered his body again and he had to be raised onto his feet.

The black stone is widely believed to be a meteorite. Islamic legends state that it was once one of the stars of Paradise.

While we cannot know for certain it is a meteorite, it is certainly the most venerated stone in the world. Every year, millions of Muslims make a *haj* or pilgrimage to Mecca and the Kaaba in search of spiritual purification.

According to Muslim tradition, the stone was originally white, but turned black from being in a world where it absorbed humanity's sins. It became impure or blackened as a result of the impurity of the human psyche. Thus, we are taking about alchemical imagery.

The black stone serves as a focal point, unifying Muslims around the world and symbolizing their common belief, spiritual focus, and quest.

The direction in which one prays is called *qibla*, which rings of the Arabic word "oalb," or "heart." This is the spiritual focus the black stone symbolizes.

Qibla also rings of the Hebrew word *kabbalah*, which means "to receive" and refers to the knowledge we receive from God. In Judaism and Christianity, this knowledge is symbolized by a ladder or a tree.

Here, we are reminded of Jacob laying his head on a stone and falling into a dream in which he saw a ladder ascending into the heavens with angels ascending and descending on either side.

In Mohammed's time, the black stone was removed during renovations. The Meccan leaders could not agree which clan should return the stone to its place. They decided to ask the next man who came through the gate to make that decision; that man was the thirty-five-year-old Mohammed.

Five years after Mohammed settled the placement of the black stone, he began to pray alone for several weeks every year in a cave named Hira on Mount Jabal al-Nour, the Mountain of Light or Mountain of Enlightenment, near Mecca.

Islamic tradition holds that during one of his visits to that cave, in the year 610, the angel Gabriel appeared to him and commanded Muhammad to recite verses that would be included in the Quran. Islamic tradition states that ten years later, in 620, Mohammed experienced the *Isra and Mi'raj*, a miraculous, night-long journey said to have occurred with the angel Gabriel.

At the journey's beginning, the *Isra*, he is said to have traveled from Mecca on a winged steed named Al Baraq to the farthest mosque.

After leading other prophets in prayer, he then ascended to heaven. During the *Mi'raj*, as it is called, Mohammad is said to have toured heaven and hell.

As Mohammed ascended the seven levels, he met the Jewish prophets along the way.

Adam was the gatekeeper of the first gate or first heaven, followed by Jesus and John at the second heaven, and Joseph at the third. At the fourth level, he met Enoch, who is named Idris in the Quran.

Aaron is at the fifth, Moses at the sixth, and Abraham at the seventh.

Idris is worth exploring before we continue. The Quran says God took him to heaven without passing through the portals of death. For this reason, he is equated with Enoch, the pre-flood sage whom the book of Genesis says "walked with God."

Idris is not only known as Enoch, but also as Hermes Trismegistus, who is credited with building the Great Pyramids of Giza, the ancient Egyptian transfiguration chambers.

According to ancient Arab genealogists, Mohammed is a direct descendant of Hermes Trismegistus. Hermes is the Greek god of communication and guide of souls through the gateways of the afterlife. His caduceus wand opens the gates of heaven.

One Greek text called *Kore Kosmou* (meaning Virgin of the World) ascribed to Hermes Trismegistus—who is also considered to be the Egyptian god, Thoth—says when souls or Divine sparks are in the human body, they are wrapped in a garment composed of the four elements: earth, air, fire, and water. The human body is constricted by these elements. This garment becomes our soul's clothes. To escape our earthly garment, mystics say, we must craft, weave, or paint a garment of rainbow light and be born again into the Rainbow Light Body.

If Mohammed is a descendent of Hermes, then these dots we just connected are saying that, in addition to having a genealogical connection, Mohammed was knowledgeable in all the matters of human transformation into a celestial being.

So now, let us return to Mohammed.

The end of his journey was called *Miraj*, which literally means "ladder." We are told Mohammed scaled the ladder to heaven. He is clearly a keeper of the secrets of Ascension.

Some interpret Mohammed's ascension to be an out-of-body experience through non-physical environments. However, from the perspective of Islamic gnostics, his ascension was considered to be an actual physical experience that included real encounters with real beings.

The seven heavens were considered objective and external from human existence. In other words, his ascension was not *allegorical* but *actual*.

Al Buraq, Mohammed's steed, is a truly fascinating creature. Its name means "lightning" or "emitting lightning." Some traditions hold that the creature had a horse's body, an angel's head, and a peacock's tail.

The peacock's tail is an important detail, as the multicolored tail is colorful and iridescent ... like a rainbow. Ancient alchemists lived for a miraculous moment called *Cauda Pavonis*, the "Tail of the Peacock," or sometimes the "Peacock Works." This moment is said to be the announcement of the completion of the Great Work of Ascension.

The peacock's tail tells us we are involved in high alchemy here. In my view, the tail is a symbol for the Rainbow Light Body.

MOHAMMED AND THE GARMENT OF LIGHT

Details derived from Merkabah mysticism are found in the famous *hadith-i-kisa* or "tradition of the garment," which tells the story of Mohammed summoning his daughter Fatima, her husband Ali, and their sons to give them a cloak. The transference of this garment is taken as his bestowal of succession upon them. They are called the People of the Cloak.

Here is the story:

Mohammed told his family members that when he was taken on his ascension journey to heaven and entered Paradise, he saw in the middle of it a palace made of red rubies. Gabriel opened the door for him and he entered it. He saw in it a house made of white pearls. He entered it and saw in the middle of it a box made of light and locked with light.

Mohammed said, "O Gabriel, what is this box and what is in it?"

Gabriel said, "O Friend of God, in it is the secret of God which God does not reveal to anyone except to him who He loves."

Mohammed asked permission to open the box.

With permission granted, Gabriel opened the box. In it, Mohammed saw spiritual poverty and a cloak.

Mohammed asked God what these were.

A voice from heaven said, "Mohammed, these are the two things which I have chosen for thee and thy people from the moment I created the two of you. These two things I do not give to anyone save those whom I love, and I have created nothing dearer than these."

When Mohammed returned from his night journey, he gave the cloak to Ali with the permission of God. Ali wore it, sewed patches on it, and passed it on to his son, Hasan, who then passed it to Husain, and then the descendants of Husayn, one after another. The *Mahdi* or Islamic Messiah will wear it when he returns. The cloak is with the Mahdi now.

This legend is also the origin of the *khiraq* or initiator cloaks worn by Sufi mystics.

A.D. 1200 ST. FRANCIS OF ASSISI

One of the most profound of the numerous post-Ascension appearances of the risen Jesus occurred in Assisi, Italy in the 13th century when he appeared to the man we now call Saint Francis. St. Francis is known as the founder of the Franciscan Order. Dante, Giotto, and Michelangelo were Franciscans.

"A sun was born into the world." With these words, in the *Divine Comedy* (Paradiso, Canto XI), Dante alludes to Francis' birth. His contemporaries viewed him in Messianic terms. He blazed a trail of light for our Ascension. Franciscan churches in Florence and Assisi, Italy have extraordinary frescoes portraying Francis ascending heavenward in a chariot held aloft by angels.

Born Giovanni di Pietro di Bernardone, Francis was raised in wealth and privilege by a father who was a cloth trader. He awoke from the dream of his upbringing, and like Jacob, traded his "rich" clothes and began the quest for the right clothes to scale the ladder to heaven. He was known as the gentle saint who spoke with birds, tamed wolves, and who turned Europe upside down. Pope Benedict called him a giant among holy men. His life arc took him from a position of wealth and privilege to self-chosen material poverty and on to the highest spiritual heights. Francis became known as "Jesus' brother" and the Second Christ to his followers.

One reason why is because they claim he lived the Sermon on the Mount better than anyone else. The Sermon on the Mount is the most famous sermon Jesus gave, and his most esoteric. In it he delivers the Beatitudes, or eight ascending steps toward attaining the blessedness of a Divine life. The eight Beatitudes, as recorded in Matthew 5: 3-10 are:

> *Blessed are*
> *... the poor in spirit, for theirs is the kingdom of heaven.*
> *... they who mourn, for they will be comforted.*
> *... the meek, for they will inherit the land.*
> *... they who hunger and thirst for righteousness, for they will be filled.*
> *... the merciful, for they will be shown mercy.*
> *... the clean of heart, for they will see God.*

... the peacemakers, for they will be called children of God.

... they who are persecuted for the sake of righteousness,

for theirs is the kingdom of heaven.

The Beatitudes describe the qualities of perfection that all who seek Ascension should embody. Scholars now know the Beatitudes found in this sermon were derived from the Essenes. Scroll 4Q525 reads:

[Blessed is] ...with a pure heart

and does not slander with his tongue.

Blessed are those who hold to her [Wisdom's] precepts

And do not hold to the ways of iniquity.

Blessed are those who rejoice in her,

And do not burst forth in ways of folly.

Blessed are those who seek her with pure hands,

And do not pursue her with a treacherous heart.

Blessed is the man who has attained Wisdom,

And walks in the Law of the Most High.

The blessed, of course, reside in the Dimension of the Blessed. Jesus is describing what life will be like in our ascended state and is calling us there.

The words of the Essene Beatitudes are attributed to the Teacher of Righteousness, the founder of the Essenes, whom they recognized as their long-awaited Messiah. Their content can also be found in the Credo of the Essenes.

Interestingly, scholars understand that the sermon, both in Jesus' original words and in Matthew's writing, was designed as an aural, memorizable meditation device. By repeating it over and over, we anchor the Ascension energies of this teaching.

As one who climbed the mountain of Ascension, by living the sermon more thoroughly than others, we may say that Francis lived the Essene way better than anyone during his time. That is a powerful and under-acknowledged statement.

Francis had a simple formula for saving mankind and for Ascension: the imitation of Christ and brotherly love. Francis transformed the church by refocusing Christians on the Gospel. He taught his followers to obey the Gospel, to care for the suffering, to preach, and to embrace poverty as their bride.

As the Mahaya Buddhists have the six paramitas or practices that lead to perfection (generosity, morality, patience, diligent effort, contemplation, and insight), so too did Francis have six practices that lead to ascension:

1. **Friendship**.
2. **Embracing the "other."** He saw the sacred in everyone and everything.
3. **Poverty**. He renounced wealth, power, and control. Being poor, Francis' way was meant to reduce the effects of karma on one's Ascension.
4. **Spirituality**. Francis showed that people can live spiritual lives all the time, not just in church.
5. **Care**. Francis taught that all of God's creation must be cared for. Francis poetically called the Sun his brother and the Moon his sister. He is the subject of The Prayer of St. Francis: "Lord, make me an instrument of Your peace." It is for this reason that he has become today's environmental saint.
6. **Death**. Francis taught his followers to welcome death.

An astounding visionary ascension experience occurred when Francis was visited by the ascended Christ as a seraphim, while in retreat in the mountains of La Verna, Italy. While praying, Francis was asking how to better please God. He opened the Bible several times, each time to the account the crucifixion.

Francis prayed: "O Lord Jesus Christ, before I die I ask you for two graces; first, that in my lifetime I may feel, as far as possible, both in my soul and body, that pain which you, sweet Lord, endured in the hour of your most bitter Passion; second, that I may feel in my heart as far as possible that excess of love which moved you, O Son of God, to suffer so cruel a Passion for us sinners."

At that moment, the ascended Christ descended from heaven as a Seraph angel with a face surpassing earthly beauty. Francis realized that the way to be made like the crucified Christ was not through suffering, but through being like Christ in mind and heart. When the vision was over, Francis realized he had the stigmata wounds of the crucifixion.

As we previously noted, the Seraphim are the angels the Essenes sought to become. The "new bodies" they sought are the same as the bodies of these beings.

In Jewish mysticism, the complete physical characteristics of a Seraphim, also known as the Watchers or Angels of the Lord, include:

- a humanoid body
- a "serpentine" face
- a many-colored garment
- a feathered cloak
- a luminous or radiant body
- many eyes
- the ability to rise up into the air like a whirlwind
- the ability to fluidly morph or change form (to shape-shift).

This is why, in Christian art, the Seraphim are portrayed as humanoid beings with swirling, vortex-shaped bodies covered with feathers. Are the feathers meant to symbolize flight, but also an energy field or waves of light emitted from these beings? I believe so. To me, the visual similarity between the Rainbow Light Body and the energetic bodies of the Seraphim is not a coincidence. Nor is it a coincidence that Ptah wore a golden feathered robe.

I have proposed that those in the Rainbow Body state and the Seraphim are the same class of enlightened celestial beings. The Tibetans haven't claimed this, and neither has the Judeo-Christian tradition. As far as I know, this is unique to me.

As they were developed in corresponding Christian theology, Seraphim are beings of pure light and pure love who have direct communication with God. As noted, they dwell at the Throne of God. However, they don't stay there. They can manifest in our world.

In fact, the resurrected Jesus appeared to St. Francis of Assisi as a Seraph, demonstrating that the state of being of the Seraph is the same as the resurrected state of being. In the art of resurrection, which is derived from eyewitness accounts, Jesus is either seen with a rainbow around his body or with the body of a Seraphim. In my view, these bodies are the interchangeable or energetic phases of the same light body. One, the Rainbow Body version, is a sped-up version of the other (the Seraphim). This is because these heavenly beings "slow down" their frequency in order to be perceived by our earthly senses.

Thomas Aquinas said the Seraphim have the quality of clarity, or brightness, which signifies that these angels have within themselves an inextinguishable light, and that they also perfectly enlighten others. With the revival of neo-Platonism in the academy formed around Lorenzo de' Medici in Renaissance Florence, the Seraphim took on a mystic role in Pico della Mirandola's "Oration on the Dignity of Man" (1487), the epitome of Renaissance thinking.

Pico took the fiery Seraphim—"they burn with the fire of charity"—as the highest models of human aspiration: "impatient of any second place, let us emulate dignity and glory. And, if we will it, we shall be inferior to them in nothing.

"In the light of intelligence, meditating upon the Creator in His work, and the work in its Creator, we shall be resplendent with the light of the Cherubim. If we burn with love for the Creator only, his consuming fire will quickly transform us into the flaming likeness of the Seraphim," the young Pico announced.

According to Renaissance thought, the Seraphim are a different type of human being, a fully transfigured being. Their "perfected" bodies are immortal bodies of light and are therefore able to hold the highest frequencies of love and light. We can become Seraphim by meditating exclusively on the love of the Creator, say Renaissance thinkers. In other words, if we perfect ourselves. The stigmata of Christ brought Francis great pain. He died within two years of his vision.

When Francis died, one of the brethren saw his soul, which was now freed from his body, wing its way toward heaven surrounded by a white cloud. It looked like a bright, shining star. This is a perfect description of the Merkaba throne or ascension throne of Christ. In fact, churches throughout Italy portray Francis ascending on a winged chariot.

1945 TO PRESENT

The Ascension knowledge floodgates opened shortly before and after the end of World War II.

Beginning in 1941 with the publication of Gershom Scholem's *Major Trends in Jewish Mysticism,* the possibility of celestial ascent and human transformation—or *apotheosis,* meaning to transform from a human to a

Divine being—transfixed a generation of scholars, who began revealing the secrets of the *Merkavah* texts. *Merkabah (or Merkavah) mysticism* is Jewish literature developed from the 1st century B.C. to the 1st centuries A.D. associated with a mystical vision of the Divine throne. The throne was sometimes envisioned as a luminous cloud, a chariot, a throne vehicle, or a *merkabah* that enabled transport between heaven and Earth.

In 1945, the Nag Hammadi library burst forth from its repository in Egypt. It was considered the archaeological find of the 20th century. Sealed in large clay jars, the Nag Hammadi library—a collection of thirteen ancient, papyrus books called *codices*—contained more than fifty texts that are often referred to as the Gnostic Gospels. These texts were once thought to have been entirely destroyed by the early Christian church in its effort to attain dominance.

Books such as the *Gospel of Thomas*, the *Gospel of Philip*, and the *Gospel of Truth* are loaded with references to human transformation and Ascension. The writers of these texts viewed the soul as having a pre-existence before becoming trapped in the matter of Earth. Salvation can be attained via a direct experience with God and seeking Ascension as a way to return to the heavenly realm of Light.

The only difference between the Christian teaching on the Ascension into a Christ body is that Christians believe one must be invited by God to receive this light garment. The "heretical" Gnostics believe humans can attain Ascension on their own. They are just like the builders of the Tower of Babel.

Many Christians believe only the true followers of Jesus will be transformed into their spiritual bodies in the Rapture, at which time they'll be translated from the Earth to be in Heaven with God.

Humans turn into angels? No way, says the Church. At least not on their own...or without God's initiative or the Church being involved. Moreover, they believe that God has a plan and a timetable for our "angelification" or glorification. Accelerating this process is forbidden, too.

At Judgment Day, Christ's sign—the Son of Man—will appear on the clouds of the sky (Matthew 24:30-36) and believers suddenly, without warning—or in some cases, without preparation— will be changed in the "twinkling of an eye" (1 Corinthians 15:51-52) into bodies that will be like Christ's glorious resurrection body (Philippians 3:20-21). Then they will disappear from Earth.

Two years after the Nag Hammadi library emerged, the Dead Sea Scrolls of the Essenes were discovered near Qumran in Israel. Between 1947 and 1956, eleven caves around Qumran yielded 900 documents. These extraordinary books tell of human encounters with angels who provide instruction on Ascension. This instruction centers on human transformation into angels (*angelification*) and Divine beings (*apotheosis*) followed by ascension to a heavenly city, the New Jerusalem, where humans sit in the congregation of the gods. While these texts are short on providing exact instructions or detailed "how to" processes for apotheosis, angelification, or Ascension, they clearly establish that Ascension was on the minds of the authors, and the knowledge was received from angels.

Like precious ancient water, these wisdom texts were also preserved in jars by the Essenes, who stored them in caves just before the Romans exterminated hundreds of thousands of Essenes and other Jews between A.D. 67 and 70. When their contents were poured out, the world was justly amazed. The conversations in these texts are astounding. They brought instant clarity to many Christian teachings.

Among the most intriguing discoveries from the Dead Sea Scrolls are the thirteen Songs of the Sabbath Sacrifice. These songs address an angelic priesthood, God on his chariot, and an elaborate, heavenly temple thronged with spiritual beings. *Songs of the Sabbath Sacrifice* describes the liturgy or ceremony which the angelic priests, the celestial beings, perform in the celestial temple.

Carol Newsom, whose *Songs of the Sabbath Sacrifice: A Critical Edition* is the definitive work on this topic, writes in her introduction: "These thirteen compositions invoke angelic praise, describe the angelic priesthood and the heavenly temple, and give an account of the worship performed on the Sabbath in the heavenly sanctuary."

The songs weren't just congregational hymns sung in praise to God; they were apparently regarded as real-time liturgical participation in the heavenly temple's Sabbath service. This means they linked the earthly Essenes with the heavenly angels.

Great care was taken to acknowledge and describe the various details of this other-worldly Divine scene, from the vestments of the angelic priesthood to the temple itself, and to the great Merkabah or chariot/throne of Yahweh.

The function of reciting the Songs of the Sabbath Sacrifice was to bring the congregation into the heavenly courts where they could participate in a Sabbath service administered by angelic priests.

Both the highly descriptive content and the carefully crafted rhetoric, says Newsom, direct the worshipper who hears the songs toward a particular kind of religious experience, a sense of being in the heavenly sanctuary and in the presence of the angelic priests.

These celestial beings are described as disembodied, non-material, and invisible. As I said earlier, I believe they are Seraphim angels.

The *Songs* were recited by the *Maskil*, a high priestly figure the Essenes "called in." His name means "Enlightener" or "Instructor." One presumes he is wearing the luminous breastplate as he recites this hymn or that his Rainbow Light Body is glowing.

As Newsom observes, the language of Song #6 to #8, at the heart of the performance, is characterized by a repetitious and hypnotic quality, suggestive of an increase in intensity of devotion.

"The performance of these songs," say scholars Rowland and Jones, "presumably combined with intensive visualization of the images described, will have had the effect of 'building' the celestial temple in the personal and collective imagination of the participants. The imperative formulae of the early hymns indicates that they are calling on the angels to participate with them in this ritual 'temple-building' project."

The congregation asks the angels in heaven (called Elohim and eternal Holy Ones), to perform their priestly duties in the celestial city while earthly Essenes imitate the spiritual activity of the angels/celestial beings on Earth. They do so to link the earthly and the heavenly realms and to receive a blessing from the angels (in Songs #6 and #8).

At the climax of the Songs (#13), the Essenes are transformed into celestial beings, high priests of the celestial temple. They don the multi-colored celestial robes of the perfect, priestly angels (celestial beings) and serve in the celestial city/temple. They join the angels in the celestial realms or intermingle with them on Earth.

This means the wearing of the multi-colored celestial robes symbolizes perfection.

I propose the angels the Essenes were living with were Seraphim and the celestial body they were teaching them about was the Rainbow Light Body.

My reading of the Dead Sea Scrolls shows that they contain the proof of this interaction and the Essene practice of human transformation or transmutation into perfect light bodies. Their goal of attaining perfection is the core power pack and red hot coal of the Seraphim found in the scrolls.

The thing is, I never really thought about the connection between the Essene light body or perfection teachings, which are both explicit and veiled in Christianity, and the defining Christian concept of being "born again."

The reason is because I am neither a Protestant nor an Evangelical Christian, the two Christian movements who have done more than the other several hundred Christian sects to illuminate the mysteries of being "born again." In Christian understanding, one is born again after proclaiming belief in only one God, being baptized in the name of Jesus Christ, and then following Jesus into the Kingdom of God.

I believe that to be "born again" means to attain the perfect light body or the Rainbow Resurrection Body. This means attaining the perfect body has the same meaning as being "born again" into a body of spirit (light, love).

Jesus told his followers—and here is the Essene Rainbow Light Body teaching—"If thou wilt be perfect (holy, whole, complete), go and sell that thou hast, and give to the poor, and thou shalt have treasure in heaven: and come and follow me" (Mat. 19:21).

In other words, Jesus is telling the rich man that if he attains the perfect light body, and is "born again," he has found Earth's greatest treasure. He then can follow Jesus through the eye of the needle (or stargate) into the Kingdom of God, where perfected humans dwell in bodies of light.

Jesus was demonstrating the light body secrets of the angels, specifically the Seraphim. Again, transformation into a Seraph / Rainbow Light Body is the same as being born again.

In some Christian movements, to be born again is to undergo a "spiritual rebirth" or a regeneration of the human spirit from the Holy Spirit. As Jesus tells us in John 3:3, no one can enter the Kingdom of Heaven unless they are in their born-again body.

The earthly body is born of flesh. The born-again Resurrection Rainbow Body is born of a spirit, a higher vibration. That holy spirit is true love.

Interestingly, the Greek word for "again" also means "from above," suggesting that the power or spirit of regeneration comes from above… possibly from the stars or the higher worlds. This means our Rainbow Body comes from and exists in a higher realm or in the stars, as the Tibetans teach.

In Christian terms, being born again is the result of a secret act of regeneration (love) by God. A mysterious power or force, the Holy Spirit, transforms our flesh-and-blood existence into a spirit-filled body and state of being.

The serpent on a pole is a symbol for the regeneration into a spirit body of the Seraphim. Again, they are considered the beings of highest love.

The Bible says that things which are visible are temporary, but things which are invisible are eternal (2 Corinthians 4:18).

In other words, those with born-again bodies are living in the eternal everywhere, everywhen, and at one with God. This is how the Tibetans define the Oneness of the Rainbow Body state of being.

This timeline demonstrates that Ascension has been a choice for humans for thousands of years. It also reveals an acceleration of humanity's Ascension experience. In the next chapter, we will explore the power of sacred art to accelerate your ascension process as we move humanity's quest into the 21st century.

THE LOST ART AND SCIENCE OF ASCENSION

———— ⊙∕⊙ ————

*H*ave you ever thought about what significance sacred art has to your spiritual practice? Why, for example, do we hang images of Christ, Mary, Shiva, or a guru in our sacred spaces?

The answer is that art, especially sacred art, has extraordinary, even cosmic, power to elevate our consciousness and to raise our spiritual frequency. It touches our souls, taps our emotions, and acts as a bridge to the Divine Self. It brings connection to a higher, purer realm and to our better, more perfect, selves. To this end, sacred art is a way for us to "call home" and to "see" ourselves home.

Mystic artists would say that contemplating, meditating, and reflecting on sacred art feeds our imagination, but it also shows us the way to our next, best self. In fact, as we will see, scientific evidence now says sacred images allow you to experience your Divinity and even to enter the Divine realm.

The purpose of sacred art is to make present the energy of the purer realms and the sacred entities who dwell there and to show us the way to attaining perfection. Sacred art differs from mundane art in that it speaks to, and awakens, an inner, spiritual part of ourselves, and pulls us to a greater cosmic reality. As George Bernard Shaw said, "You use a glass mirror to see your face; you use works of art to see your soul."

A great deal of the motivation to study sacred art comes from the Tibetan belief that just seeing images of the Rainbow Body activates our own Glory Body. The essence of the Great Perfection teaching is the direct transmission of knowledge from master to disciple. Dzogchen teaching is epitomized in three principles, known as the Three Statements of Garab Dorje:

1. Direct introduction to one's own nature.
2. Not remaining in doubt concerning this unique state.
3. Continuing to remain in this state.

Sacred art helps us to imagine or see our true nature. It is up to us to believe it is possible and to live a life in alignment with this aspect of ourselves.

As an enlightened being, a guru like Padmasambhava, has the ability to transmit the vibration of enlightenment to seekers via his physical image, which is equal to pure spirit energy.

What this means is that the images of the guru in his Rainbow Body transmit the vibrations of this perfect state.

Catholics believe the same thing about, for example, the painting "Jesus, I Trust In You." Painted in 1934 by Saint Faustina, in Belarus, this work became one of the most important in contemporary Catholicism. Jesus is shown in a white garment raising his right hand in blessing and pointing with his left hand, which rests on the Sacred Heart from which flow two rays: one red and one pale blue. Jesus reportedly asked Faustina to include the inscription "Jesus, I trust in You" with the image.

In one of her visions, Jesus said this to Saint Faustina: "I am offering people a vessel with which they are to keep coming for graces to the fountain of mercy. That vessel is this image with the signature: 'Jesus, I trust in You.'"

In her *Diary of St. Faustina* (Notebook 1, items 47 and 48), she wrote that Jesus told her: Paint an image according to the pattern you see, with the signature: "Jesus, I trust in You." I desire that this image be venerated, first in your chapel, and then throughout the world. I promise that the soul that will venerate this image will not perish.

How can this be? How can a painting transmit a Divine vibration? What is a painting but a pattern of energy? It is a collection of brush strokes on a canvas or dots on screen. When viewed, it manifests as an electro-chemical moment in the neural network of the brain. When we meditate on this image, we bring it to life in our imagination. If we believe it and live it, we become it. When we are neurochemically aligned with Buddha or Jesus, we are in a state of love, infinite gratitude, wisdom, and cosmic intelligence.

Both Buddhism and Christianity teach that the love, wisdom, and power we seek is already within us. We simply need to unload the layers of suffering and false perception that mask it. These layers are like clothes. Once we remove them and are naked, we are ready to be cleansed, baptized, and transfigured.

When we rise, and are not afraid, we live our lives based on a new set of neural connections. This changes our experience. Virtually every ancient spiritual tradition symbolizes this change as the acquisition of a white robe, symbolizing purity and love.

The images show us the way to do this. We can enter this new phase of our life, this new state of being, through the image.

ICONS: SACRED MIRRORS

An icon is a living image that functions as a two-way mirror and portal to the Divine realms. The waves of light produced by the particles of paint beaming from the icons are charged with spiritual power that rewires our brain to match the ascended mind and the perfected light bodies of the icon's subject. It also connects us with higher realities in which these figures exist.

How do they do this?

As enlightened beings, ascended avatars—like Christ, Mary, Buddha, and others—can transmit the vibration of enlightenment to seekers via their physical image, which is equal to pure spirit energy. The sacred image puts us in their energy field, their reality. They can also transmit spiritual power.

In the spiritual world, icons are images that function as sacred mirrors or portals to the Divine. In the magical, alchemical imagination of the icon makers, these images were designed to be actual doors to another world. Our world and the spiritual world are opened to each other through the icon.

The icon, the image, is the meeting place between the temporal and the eternal. This technique applies to other gurus, especially Padmasambhava in the Rainbow Body of Light.

Icons were specially created to enable a visceral encounter with a holy being. But did you know that these experiences with images can also literally take you to higher levels?

When the icons were made, alchemy was the normal way of interacting with the world. Everything was viewed as being in the process of transmutation or changing into something else, like the acorn into the oak: simultaneously unraveling and being reborn. Everything was transmutable, including the human body, which was viewed as a "pupal" form of an ascended spiritual being, usually symbolized by the butterfly and earlier by the phoenix.

"There is nothing in a caterpillar that tells you it's going to be a butterfly," said Buckminster Fuller.

There are, however, models of the "next human" or "butterfly" that is within us. These are presented in sacred icons. A remarkable spiritual technology is active and available to us through this sacred art. The transfiguration icon is a spiritual invitation for us to mirror Jesus' transformation, to activate our latent potential, and to become enlightened ones, simply by using our imagination and reflecting what we see.

This is the key benefit of the transfiguration icons.

These images were designed not just to help the early Christians to teach about the transfiguration through images, but also to encourage them to reshape their lives in accordance with the hope or expectation of transforming into light.

"Let the pose be a mirror" is a message for yogis, by yogis.

In yoga, the *asanas* are called "reflections." Many yoga studios have a feature that helps students evaluate their alignment and tendencies: mirrors. This visual aid is helpful for adjusting the body. They can take a practice to a deeper level, both physically and emotionally—especially when we send the yogi in the mirror love and encouragement.

The concept of the mirror explains the technology of icons and the practical benefit of utilizing them in your spiritual practice. The word icon comes from the Greek *eikon,* which means "image." In the New Testament, the Greek word *image* also means "likeness and portrait." Another term we might use is *projection.* The Old and New Testaments use the word "image" to describe all of us being in the image of God (Gen. 1:26, Matt. 22:20, Col. 1:15).

We are mirror images or icons of our creator. When used as a verb, the word "mirror" means "to send back or form an image of; to reflect." To mirror is also to reflect, and reflection produces insight or enlightenment. A mirror does not create images, it only transmits them. In a similar way, icons function as transmission devices. They are stations, channels, or transmitters of the energy of a flashy being and a higher vibration, the "ring" of the transfiguration that crosses time and space. Their programming code is designed to operate within the quantum human bio-computer or transfiguration system.

The materials of the image become a channel or a bridge, a gate between two worlds. In fact, to an Orthodox Christian, the images are a medium through which the energy of the transfiguration moment can be channeled, like a two-way mirror. Devotees could enter the cosmic realm through the icon.

In Buddhism, we find the concept of *ekagrata*, a one-pointed focus or concentration on sacred images. If you are deeply or single-mindedly focused on an image, there might be a moment when the forepart of your brain becomes so connected that the thought will literally become your experience.

The key is to become absolutely present with the images and to identify with the sacred entity, so much so that you become one with the images, as if it is superimposed on your being and you merge with it. This is when the metaphysics of the experience turns into the physics. Our thoughts and emotions become the body. The metaphysical becomes the physical.

Dr. Mario Martinez, a clinical psychologist who specializes in how cultural beliefs affect health and longevity, has investigated alleged cases of stigmata for the Catholic Church, the BBC, NatGeo, and the Discovery Channel. He has shown that a woman in California exhibited the stigmata marks after obsessively reading about the crucifixion.

Martinez has shown that Medieval stigmatics showed wounds on the palms of their hands because all the paintings (which were based on cultural beliefs) showed wounds on Jesus' palm. Then, science showed that Roman crucifixion specialists bypassed the main artery and hit a nerve in the wrist to ensure maximum agony that lasted for days. More recent stigmatics show the wounds in the wrist.

Martinez's theory of *biocognition* says, "Where the mind goes, the biology follows."

As we discussed, the first person to experience the stigmata was St. Francis of Assisi, who received the wounds when the resurrected Jesus appeared to him as a seraphim angel. Francis' journey took a dramatic turn in 1205 when he had a vision of the painting of a crucifix at St. Damian's church, near Assisi. The image of Christ in the crucifix miraculously spoke to Francis, saying "go repair my Church, which you see is falling completely in ruin."

The idea that a piece of art, in this case a painted crucifix, could transmit a holy message—or a sacred or spiritual energy, in this case to Francis—will later become the core idea of Renaissance art. St. Teresa of Avila claimed she received the stigmata wounds from beams of light shining from a painting of the crucifixion.

How is this possible? Today, thanks to scholarly neuroscientific work done since the 1980s, we know more than ever before about how the human brain responds to an image. Several scientists believe that the most intriguing discovery in this field is that of the mirror neuron system (MNS).

Essentially, mirror neurons respond to actions that we observe in others. The interesting part is that mirror neurons fire in the same way when we actually recreate that action ourselves. Mirror neurons fire not only when an individual performs an action, but also when the individual observes someone else make the same movement. This discovery has radically altered the way we think about our brains and ourselves, particularly our social selves.

You see a person on TV get punched in the face and you flinch, ouch, in sympathy, or when you see a loved one receiving a shot in the arm, you instinctively rub your arm. Mirror neurons appear to let us simulate not just other people's actions, but the intentions and emotions behind those actions. When you see someone smile, for example, your mirror neurons for smiling fire up, too, creating a sensation in your own mind of the feeling associated with smiling. This means our brain lights up when we watch someone smile, and we also feel them in our body.

For centuries, art theorists have commented on several forms of the human body engaging with works of art and being changed by them, but the exact brain mechanism that makes this possible was unknown.

Dr. Francesca Bacci and art historian David Freedberg note that recent research carried out on the MNS in humans, with a variety of techniques, has shown that even the observation of static images of actions lead to action simulation in the brain of the observer, through the activation of the same brain regions normally activated by execution of the observed actions.

"The observation of pictures of a hand reaching to grasp an object, or firmly holding it, activates the motor representation of grasping in the observer's brain. On the basis of these results, it is highly plausible to hypothesize that a similar motor simulation process can be induced by the observation of still images of actions carried out by other effectors."

There it is. Neuroscience is validating the spiritual technology of the icon makers! We can appreciate why mirror neurons are one of the most important discoveries in the last decade of neuroscience.

Interaction with sacred images is a form of dreaming and rehearsal for what is to come. You are connecting your brain to a new level of mind: the quantum level. Then, you are living your life from the perspective of the soul and the light body. The images show you how the great avatars exist and display our next level of being. They align us with our future selves, our future destiny.

As you contemplate, meditate, and reflect on images, you are retraining your brain to make new connections to your new self. As your nerve cells fire in response to the light of the images, they wire together or weave together a web of light that becomes the fabric or canvas for your new body of light, your new self. As you paint this canvas, you are visualizing the actual experience of the light body. You are painting a new life.

Carried to the extreme in my example, just looking at an image of Jesus' transfiguration activates our own transfiguration. It is that simple. This is how the lost art and science of Ascension works. This is why, no matter what your spiritual practice or soul advancement strategy is, sacred art can enhance your experience.

THE IMAGE OF GOD

In our journey, we have learned that many of the world's spiritual traditions tell us essentially these two things:

1. Our body was created by artistic creators.
2. It is designed to transform into a purer or more perfect form of light capable of scaling or ascending the Ladder of Divine Ascent.

Our creation, transformation, and Ascension are entwined. The key to unlocking this transformation is in the belief that we are made in the image of God and that we bear this image.

Genesis 1:26-27 records the final creative act of the sixth day of creation: Then Elohim said, "Let us make man in our image, after our likeness."

Elohim means "gods," according to scholars. This term has caused a lot of controversy among linguists and Bible readers alike. Why does the Bible describe God as "us?" Experts have reached no agreement on this.

Then, the Holy Bible says, Elohim created man in his own image; male and female he created them.

Is this saying that we look like God? Is it saying that humans are part male, part female and there are two Gods, one male and one female? You can see how this had led to controversy.

In these texts, the English word *image* translates the Hebrew word *tselem* and refers to a physical likeness of a person or thing. But this word may also refer to something beyond the physical image. This makes sense, as God is probably not a flesh-and-blood human.

This means we are not duplicates of a material being. We are images, echoes, fractals of an immaterial spiritual being temporarily brought into a flesh-and-blood state.

Perhaps it is trying to say something not about how we *look* but rather about how we *are*. We bear the image of God within us.

This spiritual image is eternal. Think about this as you read what the ancient creation accounts say about our temporal bodies or works of art.

MADE FROM CLAY

It seems that no matter where one looks around the world, most people at one time believed humans were made from clay.

"Then the Lord God formed the man of dust from the ground and breathed into his nostrils the breath of life, and the man became a living creature" (Genesis 2:7).

According to Sumerian mythology, the gods Enki or Enlil created a servant of the gods, humankind, out of clay and blood.

In Egyptian mythology, the god Khnum created human children from clay on a potter's wheel before placing them into their mother's womb. In the Babylonian creation epic *Enuma Elish*, the goddess Ninhursag created humans from clay.

According to the Qur'an[23:12–15], God created man from clay.

In Greek mythology, according to Pseudo-Apollodorus (Bibliotheca, 1.7.1), Prometheus molded men out of water and earth.

Hindu mythology tells us the mother of Ganesh, Parvati, made Ganesh from clay and turned the clay into flesh and blood.

The creation of life from clay is a miraculous birth theme that appears in world religions and mythologies from China, Egypt, Iceland, Greece, Mesopotamia, Asia, and the Americas.

In 2013, Cornell University researchers provided theoretical evidence that the creation of man from clay is actually a scientific possibility. They found that wet clay may have provided a perfect environment for life to materialize. Mud served as the first protected breeding ground needed so that the complex biochemicals that make life possible could mix.

How, exactly, these biological molecules came to mix in the first place is still a mystery, yet this finding resonates with the creation stories told all over the world.

Today's science also says this "clay" is possibly a reference to DNA, a string of data that manifests our physical body.

Where DNA itself came from is another mystery. NASA has found that the building blocks of DNA (called nucleotides) could have been made in space and delivered to earth on meteorites or by other means.

Science is now backing up what the ancients knew to be truth. We are animated bits of dust or clay, sculpted by an artistic creator with a deep knowledge of science.

Our artful creator knew about the forces of creation, the molecules of life, and must have known about DNA. This truth can be expanded into a greater Truth.

Essentially, our bodies are works of art. Sculptures. Statues. Vessels. These are the terms the ancients used to describe the human body.

During the creation of these sculptures, statues, and vessels, an *image*—another work of art—was placed in/on them.

We are now talking about two different mediums of art: images and sculptures.

Just as we are male and female, we are both image and sculpture. This is what mythologies the world over maintain.

These traditions tell us the human body, and the entire human experience, can be seen as a work of art. Earth is a grand gallery of images of God or the gods encased within vessels of clay or painted on their surfaces.

The goal of each of these traditions is for these creations to remember their artistic creator and their own artistic abilities. This remembrance triggers keys to our Ascension to eternity.

SCULPTING

The idea of our creator as a sculptor was discussed in the 3rd century by Plotinus, who was part of a movement called Neoplatonism, whose aim was to revive the light body teachings of Plato.

If we think of the image as the body of light, and clay as the body of breath, we have a perfect match.

In his collection of works, the *Enneads* I 6, 9, Plotinus writes, "Go back inside yourself and look: If you do not yet see yourself as beautiful [i.e., as participating in the Idea of Beauty], then do as the sculptor does with a statue he wants to make beautiful; he chisels away one part, and levels off another, makes one spot smooth and another clear, until he shows forth a beautiful face on the statue. Like him, remove what is superfluous, straighten what is crooked, clean up what is dark and make it bright, and never stop sculpting your own statue, until the godlike splendor of virtue shines forth to you.... If you have become this, and seen it, and become pure and alone with yourself, with nothing now preventing you from becoming one in this way, and have nothing extraneous mixed with your self... if you see that this is what you have become, then you have become a vision."

Plotinus is saying that removing the non-essential reveals to one the "godlike splendor of virtue." This technique, or spiritual exercise, does not mean modeling oneself upon another; it is not about accepting oneself as one is; it is not about willing oneself to be other than one's nature would allow; and it is not mimicry. It is about seeing one's true image.

Our true image, I propose, is our Rainbow Light Body. It is covered over by false perceptions. Discovering, uncovering, and sculpting yield the same result.

Synesius, a 4th-century Greek bishop, considered our true nature to be "something very subtle, yet material," referring to it as "the first body of the soul."

Michelangelo, perhaps history's greatest sculptor, understood this concept. Two of his most famous quotes speak directly to it:

"Every block of stone has a statue inside it and it is the task of the sculptor to discover it" and *"I saw the angel in the marble and carved until I set him free."*

For Michelangelo, the higher ideal was already present in the stone. The image of God was already in the clay. Whether this idea came from God or from the imagination of the artist is not clear. For some, it makes no difference. Michelangelo became the tool by which the new, artful being was released into the physical world.

As is also well known, Michelangelo did not ascribe to himself the ability to create his masterpieces, but only to give them birth—to reveal and liberate them out of the material prison in which they had been captive. In removing the superfluous from the marble, the sculpture, hidden there, was revealed.

Sculpture is about taking away that which conceals what God originally intended. As Divine images / beings concealed in flesh, *we* literally are the angel in the marble awaiting transformation. If this sounds like the Rainbow Light Body concept of abandonment of the material, it is because it is.

As our outer actions begin to more closely align with our higher inner selves, only the light will remain. The images or soul's beauty shines forth. This is what I was saying earlier about our quest to become not two-thirds Divine, but whole, holy, and complete.

This mindset extends to our flesh. The higher we get on the ascension path, the more we identify with our ascended self. We live our truth when we live from the perspective of our Divine Nature. We live from our Divine Nature by shedding that which is unnecessary, the dead weight. You may have never thought of decluttering your living space as an ascension activity, but that is exactly what it is.

Shedding is another important word and concept. Shedding refers to letting go. It also means emitting. The two go together in the ascension process. As we let go of (shed) old emotions, false perceptions, and ignorance, these are replaced with higher, lighter, truer light / wisdom. Gradually, the being of light within is revealed. We are illuminated, enlightened. Consequently, we shed light.

From clay to sculpting to shedding—when talking about Ascension, we always end up with the light.

Michelangelo was also a painter. One of his first masterpieces was a vibrant fresco titled *The Creation of Adam,* which can be found inside the Vatican's Sistine Chapel. The fresco is a depiction of an account from the Biblical book of Genesis of when God created the first man, Adam.

Michelangelo's Adam is portrayed as a young man with the body of a Greek athlete. His finger is extended to God to receive an infusion of soul or *neshamah.* The scene shows God transmitting the breath of life to Adam, who is in his perfect light body. We know this because at this point in the story, Adam is a perfect spirit being, clothed with an ethereal body of light. It is only after the Fall that humans were given material bodies of flesh. Michelangelo also conveys the idea of material or decaying bodies after Adam and Eve were expelled from Eden, by their transformation into middle-aged adults with wrinkles and thick bodies.

At the moment of the appearance of this fresco, Michelangelo added layer upon layer of paint to a flat surface until something that never existed suddenly appeared. Like the Creator, Michelangelo released an image from his mind. Only through layers of paint applied to the surface could it reappear.

As a sculptor, Michelangelo released the Divine from within the stone.

As a painter, he gave it light or radiance.

For visualization's sake, think of your body as the clay vessel with the image of God raised upon the surface. Think of your actions as the brushstrokes that color your light body. Ascension exercises, or expressions, include meditation, chanting, austerity, fasting, special diets, yoga, visualization, and many more. These exercises ("brushstrokes") bring self-awareness, clarity, understanding and, ultimately, self-mastery, self-realization, and remembrance that color your statue.

ASCENSION ALCHEMY

The art of Ascension has been practiced for thousands of years in tandem with the hermetic science of alchemy. Little surprise, the alchemists viewed the material body as a clay vessel animated by the spirit or soul.

While alchemical paintings may show these mysterious masters of the craft working with various glass vessels—called crucibles, retorts, and stills—the human body and image (soul) is the alchemical vessel in which the elixir of life is produced. The master of alchemy practices and works until they perfect the vessel and make the elixir.

The alchemist seeks the production of an elixir within the body that dissolves or alchemizes it into non-material light—and the personal salvation that comes from this transformation.

Alchemy is a *quest* for perfection or the raising or *ascension* of the lower (unsaved) to the saved, higher salvation.

Alchemy and Ascension are the head and tail of the Ouroboros. The alchemical symbol for this unity of all things is the serpent curving around with its tail in its mouth. It is a symbol for serenity, where the beginning is the end and the end is the beginning.

For alchemists, the goal of life is to transform our bodies of clay into a living vessel of glass. How do we do this? Easy. We fill the clay with light. The more light, the clearer the vessel. In ascension practices, the light is the Light of the Holy Spirit or Presence of God that transforms. The vessel is the sacred space or "magic bubble" in which the soul travels to its next designation.

"Clay vessels to light bodies" is another way of expressing this. Along the way, the soul is cleansed, purified, and healed (another shared goal of conscious ascenders). As the old soul "dies" in this alchemical process, a regenerated, "golden" soul takes its place at a higher level.

Artists and alchemical practitioners call their efforts "work" because awakening is not automatic; it requires that we *do* something. Sacred art works the same way. We must bring something to it: open eyes, an understanding of symbolism, a belief in a greater reality, and a spiritual intention.

The fact is, alchemy and Ascension practitioners sought the same goals, including: transmutation of base metal (souls) into gold; creation of pearls and philosopher's stones; production of healing tinctures and other substances; creation of remedies for healing every disease known to humankind; and the creation of the quintessence, the elixir of immortality, which healed, rejuvenated, and prolonged life for centuries.

In reality, the practice of Ascension is the practical aspect of alchemy.

THE HERO'S ASCENSION JOURNEY

Inanna/Ishtar. Enoch. Imhotep. Elijah. Amenhotep, Son of Hapu. Jesus. Mary Magdalene. Francis of Assisi. All are ascension heroes, masters of two worlds. They crossed the threshold between worlds and now hold open the door for us.

This next level is inhabited by these beings, and many more, who have perfected themselves on Earth or other worlds and have ascended. They began as seekers of truth and knowledge. They learned enough, and a guide entered their lives and helped them to complete their Ascension by providing essential wisdom or knowledge.

Some of their names may be obscure, but their stories are the same. All completed the journey of Ascension we are on, *while living.*

To support our heroic ascension journeys, I present my ascension-based take on Joseph Campbell's "Hero's Journey," the epic underlying story structure that all great myths follow.

According to Campbell, "a hero is someone who has given his or her life to something greater than oneself." The Tibetan Great Perfection teaching says this same thing. We do not seek the Rainbow Light Body for ourselves. We seek it for all.

The hero's journey is not just for superheroes of old, nor are the ascension stories of the past something that once upon a time happened to certain people. The hero's ascension journey is for all of us.

Every great story, like every life, has a beginning, middle, and end, followed by a new beginning. Knowing the hero's journey can make our present time more meaningful and sensible. Rather than hoping or wondering when our journey will be over, this concept can guide us through the labyrinth to a higher source of wisdom and lead us through the pain that inevitably results in our greatness.

The one goal of this process is to become more whole, holy, complete, and compassionate with an awakened heart and mind.

In my view, the hero's journey could easily, and perhaps more accurately, be called "The Human Ascension Journey." Though Campbell never discussed it in these terms or through this lens, the hero's journey is a formula for our soul's Ascension…our journey back to God.

All stories can be interpreted on six levels: *the historical, the metaphorical, the allegorical, the astronomical, the anatomical, and the anagogical.*

The anagogical is a method of mystical or spiritual interpretation of statements *or events* that detects allusions to the afterlife and Ascension. This is my specialty.

My take is further unique in that I analyzed the Gnostic ascension text, "*The Song of the Soul,*" through the lens of the hero's journey. This text is one of several "Ascension Simulation Texts" that map the awakened soul's journey and connects us to our higher self, our ascended self.

THE HERO'S JOURNEY

The hero's journey is one that Campbell brought to life in 1949 when he published his first book, *The Hero With A Thousand Faces.* Campbell traveled deep into comparative religion and mythology the world over and discovered dozens of coded stories of heroes of ancient myths told by visionaries who spoke in symbols that crossed time and cultures.

He returned with a realization that they were all the same hero. He also discovered a formula, a map, or a framework that all these stories followed. He called it the *monomyth*, or the *hero's journey*. Basically, the hero goes on an adventure, and at a critical moment or an ultimate crisis, wins a victory and then returns home transformed.

At its core, the hero's journey maps the progression of a person from a "normal" world to a higher, ascended state of consciousness. The transformation happens through a series of trials and tribulations. The stories of Buddha, Moses, and Christ all fit neatly in the framework.

The journey, like our Ascension or quest for wholeness, holiness, and completion, is often represented as a circle, because it is a cycle.

The hero's journey is a powerful tool to help us understand our soul's incarnation and cosmic travels. Even more, during a time of crisis, it provides a navigational tool. It motivates us to take extraordinary actions to ensure the victory that is before us. Think about this in terms of your own soul journey and how your birth, life, trials and tribulations, and Ascension follow this pattern.

My exploration/explanation of the hero's journey is from the viewpoint of the soul and its Ascension.

THE TWELVE STEPS

Campbell describes seventeen stages of the monomyth. However, the popularized version of the hero's journey usually has twelve steps. Generally speaking, the journeys are divided into three acts: Departure, Initiation, and Return. Let's take a look at these steps.

The hero's journey begins with the hero in his ordinary world, the comfort zone. If we think of the circular hero's journey as a clock, this is twelve o'clock.

Twelve o'clock. Our hero is restless, maybe wishing for a higher calling. Something is missing in her life, but what? Usually, she is oblivious of what is to come.

One o'clock. The hero's adventure begins when she receives a call to action, such as a threat to her safety, her family, or her way of life. It might be a phone call or an email; whatever the call is, it shakes up the ordinary world of the hero and presents a challenge, a quest, or a journey that must be undertaken.

In Campbell's research, he noted that, often, the hero refuses to accept the quest. She has fears or doubts. She prefers the comfort of home. What will people think? Or the problem ahead seems too big. Me? Turn to light?

Two o'clock. At this stage, the hero needs assistance. She is seeking courage and motivation, *something* to push her forward, upward, or outward.

This something is provided by the mentor figure, who gives her vital information. Often, this is a book or a piece of advice. This figure can be a friend, family member, colleague, or a stranger writing in a blog. The mentor figure is our angelic higher self.

Three o'clock. The hero is now ready to take the next step and act upon her call to adventure. This is known as "crossing the threshold." She leaves the known world and enters the unknown country, the faraway land. This is the moment when our soul leaves its cosmic home—call it heaven, the Pure Land, or the otherworld. The soul is originally composed of light. When it crosses the border or threshold, it leaves behind the known world and enters the unknown world of the flesh.

Four o'clock. Having left the ordinary world behind, there is no turning back.

On Earth, the hero soul must overcome challenges, travels, and tests or soul trials thrown her way on the road. Allies begin to appear, too—fellow souls, fellow wanderers, fellow seekers. The soul awakens to its predicament.

It realizes it is trapped in matter. Its powers are diminished. Campbell viewed these challenges as the food of the soul. "Opportunities to find deeper powers within ourselves come when life seems most challenging," Campbell wrote.

Five o'clock. As she progresses toward her ultimate goal, the hero approaches the inmost cave where the ultimate big battle will take place. This is where the hero gathers her forces in preparation for a big ordeal. The cave is called "the dragon's cave" or the dark night of the soul. It is the place of the soul's rebirth and the cracking of the reptilian code.

Six o'clock. The "supreme ordeal," as Campbell calls it, is where the hero faces her greatest fear or most deadly enemy and the possibility of certain death. In this crisis, she is called upon to utilize all her skills and wisdom gained from previous, smaller challenges. This doesn't have to be a negative situation. The cave could be your desk. The ordeal is staring at the phone and being afraid to call the person you just met who you know will be your future wife.

Joseph Campbell said, "The cave you fear to enter holds the treasure you seek."

What is your greatest fear? What are you dying to do that you haven't done? The promise here is that by experiencing a sort of "death," the hero can be reborn, experiencing a metaphorical resurrection that gives her even more spiritual power than before. This is the soul beginning to acquire its light body powers.

Seven o'clock. After conquering the supreme ordeal, the hero is now transformed into a new, ascended, state. She has a treasure to prove it, too. The treasure was gained by slaying the dragon in the inmost cave: soul translation. I believe the treasure is the robe of glory and the other soul apps, as these are the superpowers of the soul and are needed to be reborn. This is Padmasambhava riding on a serpent. The treasure he gained by conquering the serpent was the Rainbow Light Body.

Eight o'clock. Next comes the return home. Campbell saw that there was often one remaining test or challenge before the door to the ordinary world would open. This is where the dragon that was slayed is reborn for one last fight, or the enemy we thought was neutralized suddenly attacks or manifests. Sometimes, Campbell noted, the hero must choose between their own personal goals and a higher goal. Choosing the higher goal raises the stakes considerably. Now, with everything on the line, the hero faces her final and most powerful encounter with death.

This seems to be a test. Our mentor or higher self wants to be sure that we learned the lesson. So, a pop quiz is called. "At what point does the marathon runner know if they have trained enough for the marathon?" The answer is, "When they finish the race."

The actual marathon or race is the inmost cave for the marathon runner. It is here that all the mental, physical, emotional, and spiritual challenges are confronted and overcome. Crossing the finish line, she emerges from the cave reborn. If she is given an award, this physical token or treasure—say, a gold cup—is merely symbolic of the inner treasure, the inner gold, she has gained. The treasure is a reward for past achievement, but also a tool for future use, just as getting the golden light body and the other spiritual apps is the reward for the successful soul.

Nine o'clock. The final stage of the hero's journey is the return home. It is at this point that the hero reflects on their self-transformation. This is the Ascension. This is when the soul crosses the threshold and enters the heavenly realm.

The hero, the soul—what Campbell would now call "the master of two worlds"—has come full circle and returned to the ordinary world. But the soul is awakened and is now called a traveler. She has a story to tell and wisdom to share with the dwellers of the ordinary world.

Ten o'clock. New life. New light body. The hero has been transformed by the quest on Earth. Her soul has been upgraded.

Eleven o'clock. Everything suddenly makes sense. The reason for the journey, including all the ups and downs, and the trials and tribulations.

Twelve o'clock. The hero begins life in the new, upgraded, ordinary world.

During the hero's journey of the soul, the lowest become the highest and the highest become the lowest. What does this mean? We can think of this process in terms of school. We start out in kindergarten at the lowest point. As we grow, we go from first grade to sixth grade, from low to high. But we can't stay there, because we graduate to the next higher level, seventh grade, where we are low again, until we reach ninth grade, when we are high again. But we can't stay there either. We graduate to tenth grade, where we are low again and will be until the twelfth grade, when we really feel like we know it all.

In life, the graduation shifts are not clearly marked, but they are there. By learning to read them, we can better navigate Earth life. This is the map the hero's journey provides. If we upgrade this map to the soul level, it is equally valuable. Maybe even more so.

From this brief exploration of the hero's journey, we can see why stories are vital to our soul. If the story of a people is controlled or incomplete, it will be hard for them to move forward. Politicians refer to this as "controlling the narrative." Control the story to control the people.

Likewise, change the story and you change the people.

For example, if we are told we have no souls and that we live and we die, and that's it, then we will live one kind of life. That's the scientific viewpoint.

On the other hand, if we are told that we have a soul and that after we die, we are reborn again, we will live a different kind of life, and a different kind of culture will emerge. This is the spiritual viewpoint.

If we are told that the way to leave this eternal ring or cycle of rebirths is to ascend by living our light body as a state of being, then yet another kind of life will be lived.

That is the life the Awakened Soul is seeking.

PART TWO

*Divine Stories of Awakening the Whole
and Holy Being Within*

Who looks outside, dreams
who looks inside, awakes.

—CARL JUNG

BLUE EYES

*W*e are hard-wired to make connections between events, because connecting the dots helps support our survival. It might support our Ascension, too.

During my first trip to Egypt, I connected an amazing dot that continues to expand in significance to this day.

I was looking at an elegant, ancient Egyptian pharaoh painted on the ceiling of the temple of Hathor at Denderah, Egypt. The Ptolemaic king rides upon a boat in the stars. He holds a rod or staff called an *uas scepter*, which is some kind of mysterious, magical instrument. This scene portrays his Ascension, say Egyptologists.

The ancient Egyptians called the boat upon which he rides "the Ark of the Millions of Years" or "the Ship of Eternity." The Sun god, Ra, was said to travel through the sky on this boat, providing light to the world. As the representative of the Sun god on Earth, the pharaoh had the same capability.

The ancient Egyptians intended for us to see this as an image of the ascending pharaoh ferrying across the stars *en route* to the Orion star cluster before passing into higher dimensions (called the Fields of Aaru or the Dimension of the Blessed).

As I looked at the image of the boat, I noticed that it looked exactly like the way modern science imagines a wormhole, which is a U-shaped tunnel with each of its two ends at separate locations in space-time (i.e., different locations, different points in time, or both). The two ends are connected by a throat; they resemble the horns of trumpets or lotuses.

A wormhole is a theoretical tunnel-like passage through space-time that could create shortcuts for long journeys across the universe. Wormholes are predicted by the theory of general relativity. First proposed by Albert Einstein and Nathan Rosen in 1935, wormholes are a theoretical "bridge" through folded space-time, which might allow travelers to transverse long distances instantaneously.

The Egyptian boat, with its lotus buds on each end, and the wormhole seemed to be a perfect match.

How could this be?

It couldn't, say Egyptologists. Even though they acknowledge this is an ascension scene and the Pharaoh is traveling in the stars, it is too big of a stretch for them to see this boat as a wormhole.

However, *if* the ancient Egyptians intended for us to see this as an image of the pharaoh ferrying across the stars, then he must be in a wormhole. I mean, unless one has a spaceship, how else does one travel the stars? Theoretically, one end of the wormhole would be on Earth and the other in another place or time, perhaps the Dimension of the Blessed.

Is it possible that what the ancient Egyptians called "the Ark of the Millions of Years" is actually a wormhole, as I hypothesize?

Science says these shortcuts through space-time are only theoretical. Critics might rightly say that physical objects as giant as human beings would not be allowed to pass through a wormhole. We're too big. Therefore, my hypothesis could not be correct.

However, the pharaoh is not *in* his physical body. He is in his non-molecular light body.

My simple, but complicated, equation of the boat and the wormhole was an enormous breakthrough for me and puts an astoundingly powerful and revolutionary set of questions on the table for any who are interested in the ancient Egyptian ascension mysteries.

Did the ancient Egyptians find a practical way to use wormholes to ascend and travel into eternity? Have they left their secrets on the temple walls (and ceilings)?

Or is this just a case of synchronicity that the symbols match perfectly, both in topology and meaning? If so, which came first—the U-shaped wormhole symbol or the U-shaped earthly boat?

It is interesting how the U shape represents life itself. We all had a non-human past. We all are experiencing a present. We all will experience a non-human future. We all experienced a birth, a life, and will experience an Ascension.

After staring at the picture of the wormhole rider for literally hours, and talking about it in my presentations, I realized there might be more in Egypt that could support my growing theory. I had to find out.

In January 2002, my boots met the sand of Egypt for the first time when I had the good fortune to be an invited speaker on a tour of "the Motherland." Making a beeline for Denderah and the ascending pharaoh on the wormhole boat was the only thing on my mind. But first, we visited the Great Pyramid of Giza. Little did I know it, but this visit had an astounding ascension experience waiting for me.

Any and all who seek the ultimate secrets of Ascension must beat a trail to the Great Pyramid for answers.

Awe. Wonderment. Amazement. Astonishment. These words only begin to capture the feeling of standing at the base of the Great Pyramid in preparation for going inside.

Pyramids. Please tell me your secrets, I said from my heart (and still do every time I visit).

One of Egypt's oldest names is *ta mera*, meaning "beloved land." Mera means "the place of *Mr*" and *Mr* has been interpreted as "a canal or waterway." The hieroglyph of "Mr" is a pyramid. Noted Egyptologist Mark Lehner claims the ancient Egyptian term for "pyramid" was *MR*. He bases this on his translation of *MR* as "instrument or place of Ascension." It was from, or via, the *MR* that the Pharaoh ascended to the stars.

There we have it. One open secret of the Great Pyramid is that it is both a place *and* an instrument of Ascension. It is a mighty big tool, too. This pyramid is composed of more than two million precision-cut and precisely placed stones. To know the secret of Ascension, master the pyramid.

Surprise follows awe as one enters the pyramid through a passage blasted through the limestone. The rough walls give it a primordial, cave-like feel. The sand-covered path leads to a metal ladder. After climbing its six rungs, one then finds themselves staring into the steep, 153-foot-long Grand Gallery that leads to the King's Chamber, located near the center of the building…the place of Ascension.

Huffing and puffing our way up, my fellow visitors and I crawled through the short tunnel or passage leading into the King's Chamber. At last, we had arrived. The coolest (and also hottest) chamber in the most enigmatic space in the most powerful place in the world. We buzzed about, feeling the perfectly smooth granite walls and appreciating the smallish (compared to others) granite sarcophagus, which is the subject of immense mystery.

Finally, our buzz mellowed. We settled down for quiet time to allow for meditation and contemplation. Backing up against one of the walls, I slid down and closed my eyes.

What am I doing here? What am I going to do afterwards? It is really, really hot in here. I'm thirsty.

My mind was racing.

I took stock of where I was: in the King's Chamber of the most powerful instrument in the world, located in the center of the land masses of the planet.

Uncertain about what to do next, I opted for sending love to my family and friends back home, and then to the whole world. I visualized a wave of love emerging from within me, radiating out from the pyramid and rippling or resonating throughout the world. It was fun.

Suddenly, in my mind's eye, appeared a very large, blue eye floating above me. It was clearly sentient, and it was looking at me. It wasn't just looking. It was smiling. In fact, it was beaming bliss at me. To be honest, I was a bit annoyed. Here I was trying to beam love to the world and this distracting apparition manifests. My first reaction was, *Don't bug me, I am having too much fun.*

Oh, hello.

Then another eye appeared. They were sort of bobbing in unison as they floated above me, beaming bliss the whole time.

It was hard for me to comprehend, but these eyes were simultaneously faces. Deeply wrinkled, frighteningly ancient, living, loving, and highly conscious faces. There was nothing but compassion in their smiles. They acted as if they knew me or felt that, somehow, we were connected. I began to feel them. My arms were pulsating. They were trying to say something to me. Wait. *What?*

A slow rumble was coming my way and getting louder. Just then, a swarm of tourists buzzed into the King's Chamber.

Oh, no! The connection broke. It was time to go. I opened my eyes and blissfully left the pyramid.

When we got outside, I asked if any other guests had seen the blue eyes beaming bliss at them. No one had seen them but me.

At that moment I had the strange feeling that I would spend the rest of my life trying to return to this place and to understand what had just happened to me, along with what they were trying to say to me.

Two days later, we flew to Luxor, in Upper Egypt. After a visit to the museum, I headed for the book shop. Sitting on the shelf was a two-inch-tall plastic pyramid painted gold. In the center of the pyramid was a blue eye, exactly like the one I had been seen in the King's Chamber.

"That's it!" I shouted with excitement. "That's what I saw. That's them!"

It was the Blue Eye of Horus. It is called the *wad-jet* (meaning "whole one"). It is the logo for a race of whole and perfect beings who have ascended, who I think built the Great Pyramid.

Suddenly, everything clicked. The dots connected.

If the Great Pyramid was some kind of hardware ascension device, or an instrument, then could the blue eye be the consciousness within this place?

Are the ancients who built this place of Ascension still (t)here?

A few days later, we drove from our boat docked on the Nile in Luxor to the Hathor temple at Denderah, about two hours away. At last, I came face-to-face with the image of the elegant pharaoh on the wormhole boat that had transfixed me years before. Lying on my back. I felt like I was seeing the stars for the first time. Then, I saw it.

In the center of the ceiling is a scene in which a procession of holy ones are ascending a stairway that leads to a large orb of light (the moon) held aloft by Thoth. Inside the orb is the blue eye. Nearby, is a scene of Thoth riding upon a "wormhole boat" and holding a smaller version of the blue eye in the palm of his hand.

I was utterly astounded. There they were! The people of the blue eye. According to the ancient Egyptians, they are the elder race, and are referred to as the whole, holy, complete, and perfect ones. Egyptian creation mythology, recorded in the *Edfu Creation Texts*, says that when they first appeared on Earth, they did so as formless beings of light. Later, they morphed into physical bodies.

Had I, somehow, connected with these beings in the Great Pyramid?

The images of the "wormhole boat" and Thoth holding the blue eye at Denderah, in addition to my pyramid experience, had me thinking that Egypt had given me something special. I had, indeed, connected a major dot.

That evening, we returned to our boat in Luxor. I retreated to my cabin, feeling satisfied and fulfilled, but needing to process.

This is when I, personally, have to be very careful. It always happens that, just when I think I know something, I soon realize I don't know anything at all. In these moments, I try to "let go and let God," as they say. For example, at that moment, I didn't know it, but Egypt had sent another gift. It was already on the way. Ready. Steady.

William Henry

PILLAR OF LIGHT

, Dr. J.J. Hurtak, had a unique ascension experience many years ago where I was taken beyond this reality and given information and "knowledge" that was not of this Earth. It started during a state of deep meditation in which I was using the Sacred Names of God.

I was seeking answers to the meaning of Life itself: Do higher realities truly exist? Is there a Divine purpose for life? I had studied many books and ancient documents, and I knew that there was a greater reality behind this earthly life. I was seeking to know more.

Then, in the midst of the vibrations of this deep prayer, a morphogenetic door opened, more specifically a Pillar of Light could be seen forming in my room. It gradually grew in intensity, and a Being of Light appeared within it. He asked me if I was ready.

This was a very important moment, because as I have learned, those working with the highest forms of consciousness intelligence always respect our Free Will. Had I said "no," the experience would have stopped at that moment. However, I had enough of a background in understanding "other realities" and the experience of superluminal Light that I agreed.

Something else was important in this appearance—there was a welcoming energy presence that was so unique, peaceful, and powerful that I was accepting of its vibrations. It was clearly not of the common reality in which we live today.

At that point, my entire body was taken into the Pillar of Light with the being, who called himself Enoch, the seventh in line from Adam.

For some, this event is described as a *Merkabah* experience, but many traditional kabbalistic scholars point to the *Merkabah* as being associated with the biblical prophet Ezekiel or Elijah. The *Merkabah* is an experience of one who is "taken" into multidimensional realms by the Light Presence. It is not a vehicle for going to other local realities—that is, to the next planet, solar system or another galaxy—but of going into vast realms of life that exist in other dimensions of reality. Thus, we would define the *Merkabah* as a vehicle that can take you into other multidimensional realms through a trans-physical experience of ascension.

Yes, in my "ascension process," I saw many new realities associated with The Divine, and also came to understand many mysteries such as the geometries of the Great Pyramid and its alignment to the constellation of Orion and the star Sirius, and even the specifics of the human genetic code as part of a spiritual evolution extending to other stellar systems. I experienced the greater realms of Life beyond our third/fourth dimensional reality and acquired new thoughts regarding a higher manifestation of Life.

Once my body was inside the Pillar of Light, it was taken through specific passages or gateways—today we could call them cosmic "vortex thresholds"—not just on Earth. These are passageways or portals into greater realms of Divine Glory. I was shown sixty-four areas of scientific and spiritual disciplines that were about to take a quantum leap together, due to the spiritual/consciousness energies being given to this planet to enable us collectively, as a planetary humanity, to achieve our own ascension process.

Beyond the scenario abstracts of a multiplicity of teachings, I also "left my physical body" at a particular point. I met, in addition to Enoch, the being called *El Shaddai*, who in the Greek language is known as Metatron. He took me into even greater Divine Trinity realms.

Metatron explained that it is true that the physical body cannot stand before the Divine Presence, but the Consciousness of our Overself—we could call this our Soul-Spirit—can. Here the unity of Soul-Spirit, which in Hebrew is the *Yechidah,* the higher union, takes place where our soul establishes a higher unity with the Divine, the I AM that I AM.

I was also shown numerous other Teachers such as Melchizedek, who is said to be "fatherless and motherless." Melchizedek brought, and continues to bring, revealed information to assist our Consciousness growth. I was told that this planet had been in quarantine, which allowed us to grow and develop as a species without too many levels of interference, but that this isolation was changing and rapidly being lifted so that we would shortly come to the realization that we were living in a greater populated universal reality. This quarantine was instituted not by local levels of galactic intelligence, but by a cosmic, multidimensional intelligence that had been "watching" us—and, in a sense, guarding our development—for a long period of time. Yes, occasional levels of "teaching" interventions had manifested throughout the thousands of years of history, some directly associated with the Christ Consciousness.

We (JJ and Desiree) were together in sharing some unique manifestations after that time, and we began to work together in the midst of what we could define as the Presence of the Christ Consciousness or the Light Experience. This is the same Presence that was known to the great Teachers, from the Near East to the Far East, who continually provided Light and Wisdom to this planet.

We realize, from delving into a deeper understanding of the Light Experience, that the soul is really a wider consciousness that is temporarily here in this reality for a greater "mission" or purpose. Accordingly, the "soul" can be considered the steering mechanism or agent of change that is not limited to the physical body. Through the orchestration of consciousness, it has been placed in this space and time for a reason, and it should remain until it has fulfilled its reason for being here.

However, after that time, depending on its spiritual knowledge and consciousness awareness, the self-realized soul returns to its Overself and a new Energy Plenum is chosen. As an aware, synergistic Soul-Spirit creation, more and more of our life forces can be used for the next manifestations, moving from one level of life to another for its next transformation. Ultimately, our higher mind or Soul-Spirit unity evolves because we have an Overself or Higher Self which is also evolving.

The higher purpose of this life is to awaken to a greater consciousness awareness of other worlds with an understanding of the true nature of God, who we personally identify with the Divine Tetragrammaton: YHWH, HHYW, YWHH... in all it's manifestations.

Now we are beginning to understand the next phase of our evolution as a meta-evolution on several levels. We are also beginning to understand the powerful codes of reconnection, re-genesis, and reprogramming of our soul—our "creative mind"—that makes us capable of living in future worlds and our own ascension.

Profound, transcendental experiences await each of us if we are ready to experience them! Let us understand that the infinite universe is open and reaching out to us, as we are part of the Divine unfoldment. We can each experience the "Infinite Way" that ultimately leads to ascension. Ascension is truly the experience of "the Eternal."

Drs. J.J. and Desiree Hurtak

MEETING ON THE MOUNTAIN

a dramatic spiritual awakening had changed my life—but with the passing years, the initial wonder had begun to fade like a distant dream. The anticipation of making another quantum leap in evolution did not seem to connect with a future that I once saw so clearly.

What had happened to this exciting potential? How could I enter a new vibration of the human experience?

Sometimes I would notice a synchronicity that seemed to confirm that I was on the right path, but I hadn't felt any dramatic shifts that would make heightened states of consciousness permanently accessible. I also felt flawed in ways that I did not know how to change.

Still, I remained optimistic. I knew I needed to understand the connection between what I had envisioned of humankind's potential and what I was experiencing on the ground. If the process of ascension was taking place, it seemed so gradual that it was easy to doubt whether it was happening at all.

During a visit to Colorado, I recalled a time when my family had taken me to a place called Saint Mary's Glacier in the Rocky Mountains. Something prompted me to revisit this part of my childhood. The landscape was as beautiful and mystical as I had remembered. After a quarter-mile hike through the forest, the trail opened to a clear lake fed by the glacier. Mountains towered in front of me, and the trees around the lake looked like works of art, as if the wind had twisted and sculpted them.

I remembered well my first visit here as a pre-teen. I had scrambled toward the top of the glacier, but my mother had stopped me from climbing higher, fearful that I would slip and fall. I had perched on an outcropping of rocks overlooking the lake and vowed that one day I would return to finish the climb.

Now that day had finally come. It felt like I was living a childhood dream. As I scaled the glacier, a profound feeling enveloped me. It was as if a vast presence of love was looking in on my life from some higher realm. I felt the presence of Christ and the ascended masters. I even had a sense of my aura and my connection to the life force of the environment.

Eventually, I reached the top of the steep lower glacier, but an ice filled valley still extended before me. The landscape went on and on. I searched for something that looked like an attainable peak because I wanted a sense of having reached a summit.

A peak that came to a clear point loomed to my right. I began my ascent. With each step, I felt more connected to a spiritual presence around me. The patience, commitment, and determination required to continue climbing higher felt symbolic of my greater journey of ascension in life. Every rock and flower greeted my gaze, as if the land recognized me and was happy to see me again. Far removed from other people, I could focus on my soul's spiritual bond with the Earth.

When I reached the top, I took in the amazing, 360-degree view of the surrounding landscape. It was colder than I'd expected, and a bit windy. I sat down, leaned my back against a rock, and huddled for warmth. I stretched my T-shirt out over my knees and legs and ducked my head below the neck hole, pulling my arms inside the shirt as well. The wind was exhilarating, and I was happy to be there, even as the breeze chilled me.

After a few minutes, I heard a voice say, *Look up, I'm standing right in front of you.*

Yeah, right, I thought in disbelief. I was certain that I was physically alone on that mountain top, even though I had my face buried in my shirt and was not looking at my surroundings.

Then I heard it again. This time, the voice was more adamant.

Look up! I'm standing right in front of you!

It's too cold, I retorted telepathically. I wanted to keep my head down, craving the warmth inside my shirt, but decided to humor the voice. It felt like another person speaking directly into my mind.

Slowly, my eyes peeked up out of my shirt. There, on the mountain peak directly across from me, stood a brilliant, radiant, white flame, the size of a person. Immediately, I connected with the presence of this light and felt it was an ascended master. His light filled the vast landscape before me, though I did not imagine anyone else could see what I was witnessing. It was just the two of us.

For about twenty minutes, we stared at each other in awe of this unique and powerful moment. Our meeting seemed to be fulfilling an unknown purpose. He captivated me. The transference of consciousness that was taking place was so subtle, I found no words for it. *Who was this, and why had he chosen to appear to me?* He said nothing else to me telepathically. His silence felt deliberately mysterious. We just appreciated each other from a distance. I only know that this being felt familiar and seemed to be regarding me with great love.

I saw other flashes of color in the white flame. At one point, the being seemed to lift his arm and wave to me. A few seconds later, he disappeared. The flame winked out, and my connection to him closed. I was alone again.

Finally, I stood up. As I gazed out at the beautiful, majestic mountains, another message resonated in my mind. I felt connected to Egypt and the Great Pyramid and heard the ascended masters say, *The initiation you will go through in this life will be the greatest that you have ever achieved in any lifetime.* Their words seemed to convey an awareness that the initiation was not an experience that would happen on a single day of ascension. They were describing the work of my whole life: a journey of mastering the ascension path, instead of trying to attain ascension as a specific goal.

When I returned home from this trip, I found a handwritten letter in the mail from a woman in Germany who had recently read an article of mine. What she said astounded me. She wrote about walking in the woods when a being of white fire appeared before her. At first, she felt it was the manifestation of a Divine being.

She fell to the ground in humility and praise, saying, "It is an angel of the Lord!"

Then one of her angelic guides spoke to her: *No, that's you. Do not be afraid. That is your Divine self.*

She wrote that, for a short time, she had watched this vast being in awe, realizing she was viewing a reflection of her spiritual potential.

The synchronicity blew me away! Her story suggested something that had not occurred to me. Perhaps, the being I had seen was *me*.

That meeting on the mountain still holds a mystery, but it confirmed my life's path and restored confidence in my calling. Now, more than twenty years later, I notice each time I pass another milestone on this journey. The future seems to keep folding over to touch the past, always encouraging me to lift my gaze and continue rising to new heights.

Today whenever I doubt the dreams of my heart, I remember feeling the confirmation of a victorious future saying, *Look up. I'm standing right in front of you.*

Saryon Michael White

HOME OF MY SOUL

*I*n the Niitsitapi Blackfoot territory there is a place called Mohkinstsis, also referred to as Calgary. It was on this land, near the Rocky Mountains that I experienced an event that no one involved could ever explain.

It began in my eighteenth earth year of survival on Earth. I was on first base, minding my own business—baseball. Our team was composed of owners and clients of a hair salon, and our opponents had a less creative line of work.

I had convinced my brother to play in the outfield that late afternoon. The sun was bright and the sky's blueness engulfed my vision as I leapt up toward the clouds. The batter hit the ball with great enthusiasm for a flyball, three long strides between the pitcher's mound and me. I stretched forward and upward with my left arm completely extended to catch the ball. It would be the other team's third out.

The ball was heading straight into my glove—but just before its arrival, another glove appeared in the air above mine. Our pitcher had maneuvered himself in to snatch the ball out of the air before me.

Still pleased that we'd made the catch, I prepared to land on my feet.

But the pitcher followed my motion downwards with his buttocks leaning heavily into my chest. He crash landed directly on top of my forehead. My long, giraffe-like neck whipped my head up off the ground, and then forcefully cast it back into the dirt beneath me. I immediately recoiled like a hand bouncing off the skin of a drum.

In less than an instant, the impact propelled me to sit straight up and say, "I feel great!"

A huge smile was still beaming from my face because of the excellent play my team had just made. But before I could congratulate him, the pitcher jumped up and sped away, as though he had done something wrong.

I was ready to play again, and it would be my turn to bat. Some folks walked toward me. I assumed someone was going to reach out a hand to help me up, yet most of them began turning away from the circle they had formed around me, almost as quickly as they arrived.

I noticed their sense of timing; they moved their limbs to the feeling of grief that their eyes held. I felt great and smiled more grandly to project my joy back at them. But they looked past me. My friend and teammate approached me cautiously and I tried to ask, "Whooaa, what's with all the long faces?" As she moved closer, I repeated, "I feel great!" Her face did not budge as she continued looking straight through me. Finally, I turned to see what was behind me that kept her and everyone captivated.

There I was, still lying down on the ground. I looked at my legs, still in front of me and my torso, still lying in the patches of grass and dirt of the field. As I connected with this reality, a curtain of light was present within and around me. I began glistening in the white firmament that allowed my oneness to see the beauty of its existence. I felt no pain, no sorrow, no regret, just the pure joy of being who I AM. The peace and completeness of the space held me together. Only the sense of Being existed as I shimmered in the Light of the Light. My awareness of the beauty of this Other Side was not separate from me in any way. I was it and it was me, super-consciously connected. I suddenly understood all the answers without an inkling of a question.

This was most definitely *the* way to be me.

Time passed, but I didn't know how long I had gone missing. Settling into this new awareness, my home of homes, I understood the meaning of the sadness still emanating from the field that I once lay in, passing along in the airy mist. I began seeing the suffering like a movie, and I witnessed their distress for the body that still lay before them. I was aware of the two dimensions. The curtains became thinner until it was like I was looking through the veil of a wedding gown. I perceived moving closer to the screen. I felt no attachment, yet I appreciated and cared for every part of the pure soul of my superconscious mind and the glorious space it encompassed.

The world was calling me to come back.

By returning, I would diminish much of the suffering that connected my spirit to my body. With that notion, my being went back into my legs where I had last left them and connected back down to inside myself.

I looked back at my teammate who had just finished checking my eyelids and feeling my breath on her cheek as she leaned in to check for vital respiratory movements. Not knowing that I was in two different worlds, both perceiving and as the perceiver, she declared that she felt no pulse.

She said that I was, in fact, dead.

Still linked to—but locked out of—my body, the words, *I am alive!* came out as a shout. No cheers from the crowd ensued. Again, I closed my inner eyes and opened them again and repeated *I am alive!* Still, people continued moving farther away from the space where I lay. To them, I was unmoving. To me, the world felt so quiet. With stronger intention, I squeezed the eyes that saw the outer world shut, and then opened them, over and over again.

The clouds serenely moved the rays of sunlight above me, mesmerizing and tranquil. No air moved around my body. *I am alive!* trailed at the forefront of my thoughts but did not move my lips. I pressed my eyes shut, opened them, and closed them repeatedly from out of the blackness. Finally, I felt the air touch my lashes.

I was back in the heaviness of my bones and my blood-pulsing body. Gravity showed me the difference between the lightness of Being and the thickness of my grounded, human form. Quite unsure of whether I was noticeably alive, I struggled to sit up, hoping that all of me would rise. I took another glance behind me, just to be certain. I was all there; no parts of me were clinging to the field.

Both teams were recounting the witness of my death. Some held each other, and some told their prayers to the trees behind the backstop of the baseball field.

With no hands to guide me back up except my own, delighted to see that my legs moved with me, I planted my feet and pushed them off the soil, restoring my upright position. My eyes were grateful to see the sun beginning its descent into the freshness of evening.

Suddenly, everyone was watching me. They stood, motionless and amazed, as I walked back over to the home plate. I checked the order of my position on Mr. D's list to see who was next on deck to bat.

The whispering grew sharper all around me. I heard them.

Their eyes and words conveyed astonishment at seeing me. I was back in their world and seemed ready to play another game and win another day. They had to believe it.

Waves of relief, sighs of gratitude, and reverence for what they saw and experienced unfolding, from their own perspectives, overflowed the moment. No one felt it necessary to insist that I rest or take it easy. Nobody called the paramedics. What we had all witnessed was unmistakable and could not be minimized.

The Oneness that we experienced magically linked the people on that field and left us forever woven together. We had seen the reality of what *Is* and the possibilities of herstory embracing all places and times.

And now the strangest chapter of an inexplicable story had ended. There was nothing left for us to do but continue the game and play ball.

Clara Stewart Moore

I AM THE SISTRUM

*H*ere I am in Egypt, once again, in this embodiment anyhow, and it is a glorious place to be. The magic and mystery of this land is palpable and stories from times gone by rise from the Earth like an invisible mist. As they cocoon my body, they begin to make their way into my consciousness. I'm dizzied by the influx of information, and at the same time I drink it in like it's the most delicious elixir I've ever tasted. As I imbibe, I allow it to fill my mind and transport my spirit with intricate tales of temple life. With my psychic vision, I witness rituals, dancing, processions, and elaborate festivals. It's intoxicating. I don't want to stop, but stop I must. There is work to do, and I can't over-tax my brain.

This time, I am staying a hop, skip, and a jump from the Great Pyramid, and I'm ecstatic. My dreamtime is sure to be active, since my bed is situated so close to this powerful location. Since my spiritual awakening seven years earlier, I don't dream. In my dreamtime, I am an active participant in ethereal realms where basically anything goes. In this place in space, I receive guidance and prophetic visions. Ideally, I can learn, grow, and try not to get into too much trouble.

It's been almost two years since my last journey to Egypt and I am eager to return to a town called Abydos. It's the home of a temple of Osiris, the Egyptian God of the underworld, and the most amazing gift shop. It was kismet on the day I met a shaman at this shop who introduced me to an enchanting object called the *sistrum*. This man was built like a brick house with a round, black face and twinkling eyes. I remember him spinning around like a whirling dervish in his enormous white robe in order to present a mysterious object to me that he had secreted behind the counter.

As I gazed upon this ancient relic made of a copper-colored metal, my eyes widened to the size of saucers. Even though I'd never seen an instrument quite like this before, I knew intuitively what it was and what to do with it. This brassy object was eighteen inches long and had a long handle and a teardrop-shaped top. Thin, metal discs hung like beads through three horizontal crossbars attached inside the top loop. As my shaman friend spun back around, the discs slid to one side and emitted a sibilant and entrancing sound.

As I grabbed hold of this mystical rattle, a swoosh of energy flowed through me. Then, I began to play. I rattled up, then down, then all around, clearing his shop of energetic debris left from the last tourist group that passed through. The staccato rhythm of the sistrum punctuated by my laughs elevated the atmosphere. The place seemed lighter and brighter now, and the shaman let out a big belly laugh in delight. The sound electrified me. I didn't want to stop, but had to. My tour group was leaving, and everyone else was on the bus.

Pleased with my sistrum skills, I asked, "How much?"

He smiled like the Cheshire Cat and said, "Five hundred dollars."

"What? No!" I exclaimed. "That's too much. I thought we were friends!"

He laughed and put away *my* sistrum.

In the distance, I heard, "Time to go, Donna."

Clearly this interlude was over … for now. I bid farewell with a smug mug and a flippant comment tumbling out of my mouth: "That's okay, because I *am* the sistrum."

After a long bus ride, we arrived in Luxor. I still felt perturbed about not acquiring *my* sistrum, but I'd already moved on to my next adventure. I heard about a shop down the street from our hotel known for its treasure-filled back room. From the front, the shop looks like a tourist trap—but in the back, if invited in, you can peruse all sorts of goodies. So off I went in search of this shop, along with a soul sister. We moved swiftly down busy streets and found the shop easily. It was as if we were destined to be there. As we entered, I couldn't stop thinking, *Maybe my sistrum is here?*

Sadly, it wasn't. The store was jam-packed with crystals, statues, and other objects that my friend enjoyed examining. Feeling a little dejected, I turned my sights to an amethyst purported to be from Mount Sinai. I picked up the piece; it felt serene. It was indeed different than any I had touched before, and I liked it. It wasn't a sistrum, but it would have to do. We were almost out the door when the shopkeeper beckoned to us. He disappeared into the back room for a moment and then reappeared with a gift.

It was a tattered booklet so poorly printed you could barely see through the smudged ink stains, but what it contained was the treasure: a manual on how to shake a sistrum! Once again, I was receiving a gift from the treasure trove of life, a lesson. A lesson about patience. It's a lesson I receive often and a skill that I will master.

Now, many moons later, I'm back on this ancient land and I'm hopeful that it is time for me to receive the gift of the sistrum. I wonder: *Have I been patient enough? Did I do my due diligence with the sistrum manual I received?* I think so. I've learned quite a bit like, the sistrum can arouse passion, stimulate trance states, repel evil, awaken the soul, and annoy the temple cats.

I could feel that my shaman friend was at the shop while we were en route to Abydos. *But would he still have my sistrum?* I marched into the shop and there he stood, imposing as ever.

"Remember me?" I asked.

He laughed and nodded yes.

I asked about my sistrum and I was overjoyed when he said he still had it! He placed the instrument on the counter as I roamed around the premises. The scent of magical oils filled the air, and I began to swoon. Then I turned around to witness a woman from my group purchasing *my* sistrum!

She bought it right out from under me! My jaw dropped and she shot me a wicked look and then trotted out of the shop before I could even speak. She knew I had specifically come to this place to reunite with *my* sistrum. I scowled and looked at the storekeeper, astonished.

But instead of enacting an all-out assault upon this woman, I took a deep breath and said, "What else you got? And I want it to be better than that one!"

Once again he went behind the counter and pulled out a sistrum. I didn't like it as much. It was thinner and it didn't look as refined as the first one. It was also cheaper, only $200, but I did not care. I was crestfallen.

And just like that, everything changed. The shaman opened a bottle of amber oil and began to anoint the sistrum. I watched intently as his large hand glided over and around this sacred object, consecrating it. My eyes lit up and a big smile washed over my face. The seductive aroma of the amber was rich, and his powerful energies raced through my sistrum. When I reached out and touched it, I realized I was receiving not just an ancient device to clear energies but one that he had sanctified. I now saw an expertly crafted piece of healing technology, and I felt compelled to purchase it. As I got back on the bus this time, I chuckled and thought: *Patience does pay. It just saved me $300.*

On the final day of this journey, most of the group stayed back at the hotel to relax, but not me. I knew a job had to be done, so off I went along with four others who answered the call. Our destination was Saqqara, a necropolis on the outskirts of Cairo in the ancient capital of Memphis.

I woke early and, to my surprise, my roommate handed me a dress. I knew we'd be traipsing through the desert sands, and I wasn't keen on wearing this garment, but she insisted. It was too early for me to argue, so I donned this pretty blue, floral frock with a thigh-high slit, applied makeup that was sure to drip off my face in the 100-degree heat, and headed out.

Upon arrival, I realized I had forgotten to bring my sistrum. Getting all dolled up for the day had distracted me. *How could I forget?* I thought. I had waited so long to acquire her, and I knew I'd need her. But the sistrum was back in my hotel room, and I was in the desert, crawling through dusty tombs, dressed to the nines.

As we made our way to a newly discovered tomb, I got a sense that this was where we'd be working. Very few humans have entered this tomb in the past 4,400 years. The lapis blue and blood red paint on the walls was still vibrant and looked new. Even though the dancer scenes on the painted walls and the stories they told enthralled me, I was being called to a chamber in the distance, so I went.

I entered slowly, guided by an inner knowing of where to place my feet upon the dusty floor. Each step was like entering a code into a punch style door lock. I knew the proper sequence would open the false door at the end of this chamber. Archeologists call them "false," but I know better: They are actual gateways to other realms that I can see with my psychic vision. This imposing doorway had been carved from a single block of stone, painted brown ochre, and completely covered with glyphs.

Moments later, two of my travel buddies arrived and stood sentry, which was no small feat. I needed backup to work, and I would not feel safe without them present. Two other captivating ladies in our group distracted the temple guards, which wasn't difficult to do. One of the guards kept grabbing my bottom the entire day. Lucky for him, I had bigger fish to fry on these desert sands. Diversions and distractions come in like tidal waves on days like these, and I wasn't going to fall for it.

As I began to work, I shook — like a sistrum.

As I shook … the beaded bracelets that adorned my delicate wrists sounded like a rattlesnake about to strike.

As I shook … the entities in this chamber began to scatter.

As I shook … my kundalini snakes that reside in the base of my spine awakened to align my central channel, so I could harness more power.

As I shook … I released lifetimes of trauma that I had been holding on to.

As I shook … I began to speak the language of light, a celestial language that is ancient, angelic, *and* futuristic, often seen with one's inner vision as symbols lit with fire or illuminated with golden light.

As I shook … my hands began to draw these symbols in the air at Mach speed, penetrating the quantum field.

As I shook … I approached the gateway unencumbered and placed my hands right through the threshold in order to fortify this doorway against the lower astrals—this portal that was, in other words, a doorway to Hell. I remembered those prophetic words I'd spoken the day I didn't get what I wanted: *I am the sistrum.*

And just like that, my job was complete, and we left the chamber to go ride camels.

This journey was certainly full of lessons, culminating with the best gift of all—and it wasn't my sistrum. I realize that the sistrum is indeed a powerful implement that came into my life to help teach me that everything I need is inside me. The instrument is just a bridge to connect to the Spirit of the sistrum. I'd walked across that bridge.

I still shake my magic rattle when working with clients in my healing practice, but I don't need to. I want to. Because it's fun. I believe that's why we're here—to enjoy this embodiment and to evolve. From my adventures and seeming setbacks, I received the gift of revelation, and I now know without a doubt that I *am* the sistrum.

Donna Kuebler

DIVINELY ORCHESTRATED LEAP

*W*as I dreaming? Was I dying? My unexpected visitors defied logic and left my mind scrambling for answers.

On this ordinary night, I had busied myself with mundane tasks: unloading the dishwasher, wiping the counter tops, sweeping crumbs from the kitchen floor. I texted my college-age daughters to say goodnight.

As I fell asleep, I was oblivious to anything that might exist beyond the world I could see, touch, or experience with my ordinary human senses.

I awoke suddenly in the dark, feeling aware of my body and conscious mind in a manner I had never experienced. I also realized I could not move my body.

They were there in my room: two beings, whitish opaque with beautiful, blue eyes. I would learn later, through shamanic training, that they are called "luminous beings." They were divinely, breathtakingly beautiful. One appeared to be male, the other female.

To my surprise, I wasn't fearful of these beings and never questioned their motives. It was as if I knew them intimately from another time and place. My only anxiety during the experience was because I felt hyper-aware, but my body was paralyzed.

The beings were silent, and their gazes seemed loving.

I was still in my bed, yet around me was a void, and it was just them and me in this void. I watched them begin to form a bright, mesmerizing ball of energy between them at chest level. They seemed to create it with their minds, and it continued to acquire more power, size, and light.

When the energy ball stopped expanding, the male reached out and, with both hands, seemed to push this radiating energy into my forehead. At that time, I couldn't understand why. I thought, *Is he putting something into my brain?*

In the next moment, my body became saturated with a strong, electrical pulsing. Although it was not painful, it was incredibly intense. Upon that initial surge, I felt myself suddenly exit my physical body and then relax back down into it again. It was as if the energy had pushed me out of my body for an instant.

I stared at my two strange visitors, stunned by what happened, confused. They continued watching me intently, still lovingly, yet slightly concerned. I realized they were waiting for a reaction of some sort.

At that point, I first perceived them speaking with each other. I don't think they had planned to communicate in my presence, and I did not consider communicating with them. Looking back, I've often wondered if I could have spoken.

The conversation I recall was as follows:

Female: *We must leave her now and trust the process worked.*

Male: *No, we must try again. We must know it was successful before we leave.*

Female: (adamantly disagreeing) *She may not survive another attempt. We cannot chance that.*

Male: *We must. We need to know now. There will not be another chance.*

The female seemed worried but agreeable. Another ball of energy began to form between them. The love emanating from them was calming. I could sense her worry, though. I understood that something was supposed to transpire that didn't, and it might harm me to go through that again. It was as if they were controlling my ability to feel fear through their energy of love.

The second ball continued to grow and become more radiant and powerful. The female said, *That's enough. She can't handle full level again.*

The male agreed as he took the second energy ball in his hands.

She warned again, *She may not survive this.*

He said, *It's our only chance. We must* know *it worked.*

Then he placed the second sphere of radiating energy into my forehead. Instantly, everything in my being, everything I am, turned off like an unplugged electronic device. All I sensed at that point was static. It seemed to last for a minute or two. I had no thoughts or emotions, but I felt surrounded by static. It's as if I was non-existent in that time…

As suddenly as I was "switched off," I felt myself switch on again. I was again aware of their presence and them watching me. I heard the female exclaim with relief, *She's coming back online. She's going to make it.*

I felt myself "booting back up." It felt like a computer reset. Within that moment, I felt my physical body again, buzzing from head to toe with an energetic resonance I couldn't explain. I suddenly became aware of my physical surroundings again in my bedroom.

I'm awake! I'm breathing! The energy pulsating through me was unlike anything I'd experienced before. It was incredible and terrifying at the same time.

As my awareness of my physical surroundings returned, the beings disappeared from my perception. I could move again. Strangely, I was already sitting up in bed with my arms straight out in front of me and my palms facing my bedroom ceiling. An intense energy pulsated through my body and was jetting *from* my body. I could see energy surging from my palms.

I'm not concerned about the insane fact I can see this energy with my physical eyes. I'm simply terrified to move my hands, afraid I may harm something with this energy, I thought.

I knew that they had somehow placed me in this position—sitting upright with my palms facing up—before I woke up. I wondered if this was to protect me, my surroundings, or both. In hindsight, it's as if they knew I'd be frightened and positioned me in a way that let me explore that fear first.

I tried to process it. Staring at this energy flowing from my palms, I'm terrified and searching for answers with my logical mind.

Paranoia moved in next. *Is this real?* I thought about the super-hero and science fiction movies I'd seen. *Were they real? Is something coming to get me?*

I wondered briefly if I should write a goodbye note to my children.

I felt I had changed forever. I was so different now that, if I ever returned to my normal life, people would notice.

I sat there in bed, frozen, for fifteen minutes, considering every rational explanation for what I'd experienced. When I found nothing, my mind went to a space I didn't know well, on the other side of rationality and logic. My visit from the luminous beings had been paranormal, not logical. The energy continued pulsating throughout my body and flowing from my palms. I could still see it: millions of little sparkles shooting straight upward to the ceiling.

I had never been so energized or so terrified.

I began catching my breath. Even my breathing felt strange. I started moving my hands carefully, to see if the energy affected any part of my environment. It didn't seem so. I finally mustered enough courage to get out of bed and venture to the kitchen. *I need to do something normal.* I sat for hours snacking on cookies and milk, searching on Google while wondering if investigators would later check my search history.

Nothing I found online compared to my experience except science fiction. I was still terrified someone would eventually show up at my door to interrogate me about these strange visitors. I wanted to wake up my daughters, but I didn't want to scare them. I also didn't want them to think I was crazy. I'd been a rock for them growing up.

I knew I was sane, but how could I explain this in a way that didn't *sound* crazy?

When the shaking wore off and I was full of cookies, my mind was exhausted. I walked back down that long hallway to the place it had happened, crawled into bed, and cried myself to sleep. I'm not one to cry, but I was so confused. I whispered to myself: *I am a logical, rational human being.*

The six o'clock alarm sounded, and I groggily went through a mental routine: *Awake, check. Alive, check.*

Scared, check.

Was it all a dream?

My body and my palms were still tingling, although to a lesser degree. Had I really received a visit from luminous beings that left me shaken, frantically searching for answers online in the middle of the night? Or had I just had the strangest and most vivid dream of my life?

I remembered my midnight snack and realized I had a way to find out.

If I'd been visited by beings and charged with special energy, I would need to devote the rest of my life to discovering what unique gifts I now possessed.

If it had been a dream, I'd figure out a way to shake it off and continue my current life.

I tip-toed into the kitchen and found my proof. The empty glass and cookie package were still there.

Julia Eiler

OPENING TO THE MERKABA

*I*n the early days of my Akashic Records practice, my guides tried to train me to be comfortable with change. Before I learned to trust the process, this dynamism frustrated me. I longed for security and stability in a sacred space.

In my meditations, I envisioned myself standing by a specific tree and doorway, in an effort to build a consistent bridge to my inner guidance. The tree eventually began to vary in kind, now deciduous, now evergreen. It was as if they were playfully inviting me to keep breathing through the unexpected and find delight in surprise. One day, the tree appeared as a palm. From under its fronds, I followed a sandy path to the seashore, where I felt the ground shifting beneath my feet.

I laughed at my meager attempts to freeze infinity just so my mind could enjoy a measure of control.

Waving the white flag, I gave myself more deeply to the flow of Divine Intelligence and opened to greater possibility in my practice. Shortly thereafter, the tree and the doorway disappeared altogether. My guides had replaced them with a great crystal tower, which they informed me would act as a more stable portal for my connection.

And then, one day, the doorway returned—this time disconcertingly narrow. I felt this was a bad sign, but I couldn't determine the meaning or function of the narrow doorway. I did the next best thing: I left the question open to the ethers, so the answer could come to me when I was ready to receive it. All I needed to do now was relax into quiet awareness.

Within a couple of days, I found myself watching a video on something called the "light body"—a phrase not wholly unfamiliar to me, but which I scarcely grasped. Minutes into the video, words jumped from the screen directly to my consciousness:

"Straight is the crossing point and narrow is the way that leads to it."—*Epic of Gilgamesh*

"Enter through the narrow gate. For the gate is wide and the road broad that leads to destruction, and there are many who go through it. How narrow is the gate and difficult the road that leads to life, and few find it."—Matthew 7:13-14

I recognized this was an answer to my question concerning the shift in my connection, so I made notes and watched the rest of the video, which presented the light body as a type of celestial vehicle that allowed the consciousness to rise to the heavens. The concepts rang hollow at the time, but I knew I was opening to something on another level.

Specifically, I recognized a thread I had dropped a few months earlier, when my guides showed me the shape of a donut and dropped the word "Merkaba" into my consciousness without further elaboration. I took the left-brained approach of purchasing a book by a recognized authoritative source of information on the topic. I read it with some interest and learned that the donut shape I had seen in my visions was called a *torus*, and that it was somehow related to the *Mer-ka-ba*—which means literally, the "light-spirit-body."

Still, the concepts remained opaque to me in their abstraction, and the exercises struck me as overly complicated. Having to count my breaths and force my visualizations into a template felt like I was trying to bring about an organic event through entirely artificial means. Having spiraled back to this event, I returned to the exercises, but found myself getting no further than I had before. Disappointed and trying not to feel like a failure, I let the matter drop once more, trusting that another piece of the puzzle would eventually come my way.

Two days after my unsuccessful attempt at activating my Merkaba, something monumental happened: I finally left the teacher who had first introduced me to the Akashic Records, because it had become painfully apparent that our relationship had run its course. Although endings are inherently uncomfortable experiences, I felt ready to endow my inner teacher with all the authority I had long externalized and projected onto others. As the calendar year started winding down into winter, I felt a new mantra come in, beckoning me "to experience the Divinity within and live in the magic of the world."

I felt the nudge to travel abroad late in April—a time of year I didn't usually set aside for vacations. But the call was loud and clear enough that, without any opinions, wants, or preconceptions, my husband Brian and I opened a world map to explore possible destinations. We both felt drawn to the Yucatan Peninsula, where neither of us had ever been. After a bit of research, we booked a ten-day stay and wondered what this adventure would bring. All our past vacations had been born of specific desires to see certain parts of the world based on what we had read or heard from others' experiences. Something about this trip felt different.

I asked for guidance on anything I should know or prepare for. The first thing my guides suggested was to undergo a Temazcal ceremony early on to cleanse and open myself for the rest of the journey. Then they showed me images of rocks and directed me to find some ruins. I practically laughed in their faces. The Yucatan abounded in Mayan ruins. Could they be more specific?

Find ones that haven't been fully restored, was as precise as they would get. But they added that I would feel a connection deep within my sacral chakra when I stumbled upon a spot replete with Earth energy. There would be deep recognition, they explained, because I had chosen the location myself in a past life. That version of myself imbued the rocks with memory, and I now needed to travel there physically to "pick that package up."

Intrigued, mystified, excited, and a bit nervous, I arranged for a ceremony on the very first morning in Mexico. I set a deep intention to hold my faith that everything else would fall into place because "everything was always working out for the best." I kept reminding myself that I could not mess this up, though of course, thoughts of that very sort cycled periodically through my mind.

What if I don't find the right set of ruins?

What if I can't find my spot?

What if I don't know what to do once I get there?

What if nothing happens?

Every time those intrusive thoughts popped up, I would take the opportunity to reconnect with my breath and my soul's intention.

We hadn't even left the Mérida-Rejón airport when I faced a test. The rental car that Brian arranged to pick up was exorbitantly more expensive than initially quoted, and the new price did not sit well with him. He insisted on taking a bus to our accommodations instead and catching another bus to the ceremonial site the following morning. Yet we could not find a convenient bus route to the sweat lodge, and my anxiety grew. *If I missed my appointment, would I be "pure enough" for the rest of the trip?*

My husband turned to me and gently reminded me of my intention. "Everything is always working out for the best, remember?"

After a bit more research, we found a rental company right in town with lower rates than we originally intended to pay, and everything did indeed work out for the best.

Off on our journey, I developed a sense that the rocks I sought were in Ek' Balam, a site considered off the beaten path. Because we were making our way across the Yucatan from west to east, we wouldn't get there till the tail end of our trip. Day by day, even while learning and having fun, I felt anticipation building. The moon grew full on the eve of our visit to Ek' Balam, and I awoke feeling supercharged in the morning. Brian described me as a freight train barreling forward from the moment I hopped out of bed. Like a drill sergeant, I kept him moving at a quick pace to ensure we were first to arrive at the parking lot. Tickets in hand, I led the way to the top of the Acropolis, the crown jewel of Ek' Balam.

I knew my special place wouldn't be so obvious as that, but I wanted to be the first to summit so I could take in a 360-degree view of the site in solitude. It was a thrilling moment—yet I was none the wiser as to where I should head next. We continued exploring the grounds while I opened my inner senses. Doubt and anxiety were worrying the edges of my consciousness, but I continued to hold my breath steady.

Nearing the end of our rounds, we walked up a minor structure. At the top, I felt nothing. Brian wandered off to photograph birds while I stayed behind wondering what to do in the meantime.

Then I turned a corner and caught sight of some crooked steps amid the roots of a small tree. Raising my gaze, I spotted a large tree across the way. A sense of home filled my heart. I sat and dropped into meditation and relaxed into the arms of the Great Mother.

Over the last few days of our trip, weaving through plazas and sacred groves, I felt the stirring of a great shift. It came to me in soft, sweet whispers:

There's a different way.

A new life awaits.

Small and simple.

Time to move.

And everywhere about me I saw evidence of this in so many old women who carried the peace and wisdom of the Cosmic Mother. They emanated a quiet Divinity from the sidewalks, market stalls, and anonymous corners of Valladolid.

A shift occurred and I found my security and stability in a sacred space.

Ysette Roces Guevara, Ph.D.

UBIQUITOUS NATURE OF LOVE

I've been clearing debris from my mind for fifty years, or maybe it's been lifetimes. I've gone through many different healing modalities, each one chipping away layer of unspoken grief for an emotionally tortured and neglected life. I couldn't even touch my anger until well into my adult life, and when I did, it made me sick.

My mind gained its strength in supporting my many errors in thinking with a ritual of self-abuse that I had become excellent in executing, the price for all the years of feeling worthless and not good enough. I manifested and delivered to myself more of the same, as proof of my worthlessness. Life delivers what the mind decides.

After twenty years of immersing myself in various methodologies, books, retreats, and teachings, the idea that I was wrong in my assessment of myself started sinking in. It was pointing me in another direction. Oh, but how I clung to all I knew, no matter how it hurt me.

One day after attending another weeklong spiritual retreat, I was waiting for a mentoring call. I'd take part in these calls once a month, to help keep my mind from defaulting into its familiar patterns. I was sitting there thinking that I had not done my homework. I wasn't eating very well, I wasn't meditating, and that was all it took to send me back into a past where I was never going to get it right, I was not good enough, and love was always going to be just out of reach, no matter how hard I tried.

Within milliseconds, the hormones and brain chemicals were right there, supporting my mind's accustomed rhetoric of "not good enough." I was lost in it, and I fell deeper into the bottomless pit inside me. As I wallowed in the twenty-year-old, well-perfected behavior of self-cruelty, something extraordinary happened.

A *Christed* version of myself spoke through me.

I was never a religious person and according to my weak, influenced understanding of religion, I was born into sin. Only through baptism or acts of contrition could God cleanse my small, insignificant, sinful life. I felt ashamed and hopeless.

Something opened inside me, and I felt I understood Christ's true message in a way not interpreted by the men of God. My heart overflowed with compassion, forgiveness, and love I had never experienced before.

What I understood in that moment was that there was nothing I had to do, and nowhere I had to go, for the love that lives inside of me.

All my choices about eating, meditating, or anything else are optional, although these practices support this body and mind tremendously. Still, I didn't need to do anything at all. I didn't need to add to what was already inside of me. I cried as I sank into this truth, which felt like a soothing balm to the emotionally unattended, miserable life I had been living. I felt that love was being generated from deep inside existence itself. It was a new experience for me, and in a moment, I felt an intuitive knowing from a place I had never been.

A lifetime of explicit self-abasement vanished in a single moment. This profound change carried me through more than a decade of ever-increasing, incremental consciousness expansion.

Over these last twelve years, I would remember and then forget again. So, I went looking for the depth I thought I still hadn't reached. One night during the intense energies of a super full moon, I was compelled to build a sacramental fire. I opened with a prayer to invite all primordial energies and guidance to aid in this process of releasing and to help me to become aware of my higher purpose. I wanted to let go of whatever was still lingering in my subconsciousness that continued to stop me from fully being present in my life and connecting with others. Using sticks as an extension of my heart's wishes, I blew love into them to honor what I needed to let go of; things that had served my survival at one point.

A week later, it was like the floodgates to my soul flew open. I built a website, which I had never done before, and started posting my newly found voice by writing short, daily meditation pieces.

I have hidden inside my life out of a fear of being vulnerable. Fear still rears its head, but I keep diving off the cliffs of my life, learning to leap in the faith that I have always been cared for. I believe I will remain surrounded by and caught in an invisible network of love made up of the interconnections between plants, animals, weather, stars, planets, and the ever-shifting energies of all that is. I had never seen these interrelationships inside myself before.

I discovered, under that full moon, that I had deep intuition. I just hadn't been listening to it. This second activation somehow opened my energy flow. I found a way to allow the present moment to work through me by following the signs the world shows me.

What a gift it has been. Love is living through me, as me, guiding me into a life on fire with enthusiasm and excitement, pulled by my soul to follow the heart of my intuition into a story of courage, expansion, and love expressed.

Susie Cassaro

THE DIVINE SOURCE WITHIN

I was nearing the end of my undergraduate studies and preparing for final exams. For weeks, my life had been stressful as I juggled my time between collegiate demands and working the lunch and dinner shifts in a local gourmet restaurant. One Friday night as I finished the dinner shift, I began to experience an almost unbearable stomach pain. The pain was so intense that it left me doubled over and panting for breath.

My concerned coworkers offered to take my tables so I could go home. Suddenly I felt an almost imperceptible "pop" in my mid-section, and miraculously, the pain was gone! I finished out my shift and called it a night.

When I awoke the next morning, I felt queasy and lethargic; however, I had invited a good friend to my house that day with the promise to dig daylilies from my garden as an early birthday gift. I had no option but to rise from my bed and somehow find the fortitude to persevere.

With each downward thrust of my foot on the spade, I felt overwhelmed with breathlessness and fatigue, but somehow, I managed to disentangle the lilies' roots from the southern red clay. I placed the bare rhizomes in the three decorative planters I had filled earlier with black, fertile soil.

My friend was pleased with her gift. She joyously loaded the planters into her car and departed for her own garden. I had maintained a strong demeanor for my friend, but as soon as I saw the taillights of her car exit the driveway, I stumbled back inside my house and fell onto the sofa. I lay there for what seemed an eternity, feeling nauseous and somewhat disassociated from my surroundings.

Later in the day, my husband returned home and reminded me of our dinner engagement that evening at a French cuisine restaurant. Not wanting to disappoint my husband, nor the friends we planned to meet, I roused myself and prepared for the evening out. The *maître de* escorted us to our table, where we met a group of six enthusiastic diners and a table peppered with bottles of red and white wines. I was offered a glass of Merlot and readily accepted it.

I surveyed the menu's multitude of delectable choices and soon settled on the crispy duck breast topped with a cherry crème anglaise. I nibbled on my dinner and sipped the wine but drank water as though I had just survived a trek through the Sahara.

Upon returning home, I felt sick. I ran to the bathroom and began throwing-up everything I had consumed at dinner. I called to my husband and asked if he thought the red in the mix might be blood, but we both recalled the duck with cherries and the glass of Merlot. We rationalized away the idea of blood and retired to our bed.

The alarm clock rudely blasted me awake at 6:30 the next morning. I had a throbbing head and a thirst beyond anything I had ever experienced. My husband bounded from bed, chatting enthusiastically about the great treasures we would find at a nearby antique flea market. I had planned to attend the market but declined due to my intense headache. He chuckled, saying I should not have had all that wine the night before, although I'd barely finished one glass. He acquiesced with my decision to stay home and headed downstairs to prepare to go without me. As I lay in bed, my thirst overwhelmed me. I struggled out of bed, leaned over the staircase railing, and called downstairs asking for a soda. When I turned from the railing and entered the bathroom, it was lights out!

My eyes must be deceiving me as I have never seen anything so incredibly beautiful! I thought. The snow-capped mountain range across the vast, green valley was breathtaking and spanned the horizon as far as I could see. The sky above the mountains was such a deep blue, it appeared to be verging on the Kármán Line, the outer limits of Earth's atmosphere. I looked down and found myself standing on a mountain range on the other side of the valley. The greenness below me reminded me of an emerald—that rare, deep-green, precious gem that symbolizes balance and harmony.

I was one with the environment, feeling more alive and renewed than ever before! I was happy and calm with a sense of clarity beyond human description as these feelings overwhelmed me. I knew I would never be the same. At last, I had returned to my primordial spiritual home of pure energy and love.

As my senses adjusted to the surroundings, I focused on a huge tree, one I'd not seen before. How could I have missed it? It stood majestically in the middle of that emerald valley. The tree spoke to me! It was the Tree of Life. I looked down from my mountainside perch and the tree—with its loving, outspread arms—beckoned me to come and stand beneath it. In a flash, I was there on the ground with the tree enveloping me in its loving spirit.

However, I was not alone. Animals surrounded me. I was engulfed in a melodious choir of animal voices singing, "Behold the beauty of life!" Flooded with emotion I saw birds, deer, rabbits, squirrels, elephants, lions, tigers, cats, dogs, and every animal possible.

And there stood Holly, my fourteen-year-old Rottweiler who had passed away peacefully in my arms only a few nights before! But she was young, maybe two or three years old, strong and upright, her little nub of a tail wagging so hard it made her hips wag, too. She ran to me, and I fell to my knees, holding her face in my hands, showering her with kisses and tears as she licked my face and smiled at me. My soul was fully and completely aware at that moment. I knew I was at last where I belonged, in the all-knowing realm, where life truly begins.

As I knelt before my dog, far, far away in the distance, I could hear my name. *Who could that be? What do they want?* As I listened intently, the voice became louder and more insistent, calling me again. I was becoming rather annoyed. *Why was this person disrupting my peaceful experience in this beautiful, loved-filled realm?* I listened closely and soon realized it was my husband's voice, now sounding frantic and loud, shouting at me.

I tried to resist his voice. I did not want to acknowledge him, but he sounded afraid, and I decided to listen in earnest. As soon as I gave in to him, I felt myself shoot upwards, leaving the safety of my tree and the beautiful animals and the lovely green valley receding farther and farther into the distance.

My eyes fluttered open and my husband said, "Don't move! An ambulance is on its way."

The stairs creaked as an army of paramedics made their way to the second-floor bedroom. I felt a sudden coldness on my chest as technicians put ECG leads into place and a tightening on my arm as the blood pressure cuff began to inflate. Multiple voices were barking out numbers as rescuers lifted me from the bed onto the gurney.

"Hang in there! You are going to be okay," my husband reassured me as they wheeled me down the walkway and out to the gravel drive where the ambulance waited.

Thankfully, on that fateful Sunday morning, my husband heard me fall as I went into the upstairs bathroom. He had found me on the bathroom floor, unresponsive, eyes set, not breathing. Quickly carrying me to the bed, he dialed 9-1-1, and began to perform CPR, not realizing I was far away and completely unaware of anything on the earthly plane.

A full week had passed since my stomach pain first occurred. As it turned out, the "pop" I had felt that night at work had been a blood vessel from a perforated ulcer bursting in my stomach. I'd lost a significant amount of blood over a thirty-six-hour period; to be exact, I lost over more than 30 percent of my blood volume. I coded twice in the ER. The treating physician informed me my situation was touch-and-go due to my blood loss. My rare blood type, A negative, was in short supply and had proven difficult to find.

Following a three-day stay in the ICU and two days in standard care, the hospital discharged me to my home.

It was a beautiful, clear spring day and I felt happy to be alive! I savored every minute of the drive home, commenting on the lovely homes and gardens as we passed through familiar neighborhoods, finally winding our way home and into the driveway. The beauty in my yard overwhelmed me. Never before had I seen the flowers, trees, and wildlife the way I was now seeing them. Everything shimmered and vibrated. I stopped at each flowering plant along the walkway and held it in my hands.

"Can't you see the energy coming from the leaves? Can't you hear them?" I exclaimed over and over.

My husband kept tugging at me, anxious to get me inside and into bed, but I could not stop marveling at the "life" I could see and hear emanating from everything.

I had changed, physiologically, mentally, and spiritually. My life in the time before my near-death experience (NDE) had been one of strangeness and synchronicity since early childhood. But in the weeks and months following my NDE, I developed a noticeable increase in my intuition, precognition, and psychic dreams. I also experienced an energetic alteration in my physiology that resulted in blown light bulbs each time I turned on a lamp, touched a light switch, or walked under a streetlight. At the grocery store, I could no longer take cans from the shelf because doing so caused an electric shock and often an audible snap and visible spark. My hands had become electrified!

My life since the NDE has been electric, too. My heart is full of gratitude and joy for this soul-level awakening.

Pamela Nance

BENDS IN ETERNAL AND EVERYDAY TIME

We left the gold of inland sunshine to journey to a rented cottage on the grey and silver coast in mid-summer. Our rustic, temporary home rested on a hill deep in an old-growth spruce forest above the sea. After the first day, the steady drum of the waves worked its magic to slow and syncopate with our heartbeats. We settled in and spent days walking the shore or tucked back into the dunes, out of the chilly wind.

One late afternoon, I walked to the cabin alone to make dinner. Jim lingered on the beach. My night-owl husband would eat much later. Once I'd cooked and eaten the spaghetti, I walked over the uneven floor to gaze west through the wall of windows. I could see the shades of color and texture gracing this adored place. Dark and pale greens, steel-blue sea, and a lavender horizon spread out before me. Looking down through the woods, past the shrubs, the dunes open onto a vast plane of sand. Standing on the dove-grey sand, my husband, Jim, stood with his back to me. It seemed a long time that he meditated on the rhythmic tide.

What was occurring in his inner world of thoughts and feelings? What messages was he hearing? I smiled when, characteristically, he shook his hands to warm them. Then he turned around and began to walk up the path.

Jim is easily recognizable. Like a dancer, he is slim and athletic. He has shoulder-length hair. His monochromatic dark clothing and the graceful cadence of his movements are emblematic. He entered the shrubs leading into the forest and was no longer visible, absorbed into the dense green. It's a short, nearly straight, uphill hike to the cottage and for Jim, without my company to slow him, it was a five-to-seven-minute stroll.

Eager to reunite, I went out through the glass doors adjoining the picture windows and onto the big, tilting deck. When Jim emerged just below the deck railing, I would wave and yell "Welcome home!" or something teasing at him. Beaming, I waited to lean over the railing—but no Jim appeared.

I waited longer. Something was amiss.

A strange mix of dread, loss, and wonder filled me. It was not only bizarre that he hadn't yet arrived, but there was also a change in the atmosphere. The giant trees leaned in, their presence intensifying. The waves sang louder, and the air felt lighter, as if infused with helium. Everything around me changed. It felt like the molecules that bind us into form had loosened. The chair, wooden beams, and porch were somehow less solid. I felt disoriented, a bit dizzy, and untethered. I thought I might float away.

Alarmed by a racing heartbeat and moisture dampening my forehead—along with resistance to what was unfolding—my mind grasped for explanations. As I paced the room, reasonable possibilities arose. *Perhaps my husband has wandered off the path to explore one of the short side trails. He might be admiring a giant tree or returning to the beach. Or am I at the beginning of an illness that has skewed my perceptions?*

But rationalizing could not override what I sensed in body and soul. Inexplicably, everyday reality had shifted. Eternal time and space had opened up new possibilities. Agitated, I decided to move and to seek resolution.

I walked down the path to find him. The forest was a witness.

I couldn't find Jim in the woods, on the beach, or down the shoreline. No one was visible. The salty air permeated my body. I sighed and took a deep in-breath—and a liberation transpired. It felt like the first inhalation of a newborn. My thoughts quieted and the world no longer felt discordant, but serene and resonant. All would be well.

I walked back to the house, washed the dishes, and cleaned up the kitchen. Then, peacefully, I settled on the velour orange couch in the living room and read.

About half an hour later, I heard the back door open and Jim ambled in. To get his immediate attention, I rose swiftly and stood in front of him.

"Something bizarre happened, and I want to tell you," I said.

His eyes widened, and he stood attentive and close. I didn't expect rational answers to my questions but, in a performative way, I asked them anyway. "Why did you start up the path earlier but not come home? How long ago did you leave the dunes? Did you stand in the sand and look out, watching the ocean, before you left the beach?"

Jim explained he had not started up the path. He had been on the beach contemplating the sea before heading to our temporary home—but he'd taken a different route back, from farther down the shore.

"I think I entered a rift in space and time—an unexpected place between worlds," I told him.

Accustomed to my spiritual sojourns, he listened without skepticism.

For that night and our remaining time at the coast, a sense of smallness smiled in my heart. The awe of the encounter had left me more aware of the mysteries of the universe. The experience was humbling and a blessing, because it opened a fluid, vast sense of reality for me.

Dr. Joanne Halverson

COMPASSION AND HEALING OF CHRIST

*A*lone in Chile, unable to speak Spanish, I have left my traveling companions behind in Peru. My group tour has been canceled and I now have three days in Santiago City before I can continue my journey.

I decide to take in the sights and find a private tour of this famous city.

My personal guide, Mattias, is a gregarious man in his mid-twenties. Thankfully, he speaks excellent English. I share that I have just come from Peru, where I had participated in ayahuasca ceremonies to assist in healing my medical condition: a primary immune deficiency. Mattias immediately leans in closer to me, raising his eyebrows in curiosity as we weave through the city streets together. Talking quickly and excitedly, he tells me he is beginning his own practices in energy and spiritual healing.

Eagerly I share my stories of illness and healing, including my recent research on the role of the wounded healer, while training as a counselor. As we speak, a close and trusting bond forms between us. However, I know that I am here to see the city sights and outer landscapes—not just talk about inner landscapes.

I feel safe with Mattias as we explore Santiago's central Plaza de Armas. The Plaza's imposing, historic buildings of white stone were arranged in grand, neo-classical architectural style. Decorative, Baroque, carved-stone towers with turrets grace the rooftops. They look like icing decorations dressing up a large, plain cake and the place exudes a powerful external beauty.

But that beauty contradicts the plaza's violent past. I remember the ugly assassination of President Allende in 1973 in the Presidential Palace, which borders the plaza. Walking past his bronze memorial statue brings those associations with bloodshed into my awareness. Mattias is talking about the long history of violence against the indigenous peoples.

Looking for refuge from the bustle of the plaza, we step under the elaborate portico and through the thick, wooden carved doors of Santiago's Metropolitan Cathedral. This church is dedicated to the Assumption of Mary into Heaven and serves as the home of Chile's Catholic Archdiocese.

I immediately enter a world of silence. Muted, soft light and shadows of candlelight play on the light brown, stone walls. The marble columns and white stone foundations are offset with sumptuous, carved gold decorations. Unfurling above us, like waves rippling out across the ocean, high ceiling arches stretch far into the distance toward the main altar. Between the ribs of each arch, sky blue and white clouds encircle frescoes of saints, to contrast against the ornate gold surrounds.

Wrapped in a cloak of sacredness I reverently circumambulate the cathedral's side chapels. Mattias keeps a respectful distance behind me. He is now silent in response to the hushed atmosphere, but still accompanying me and waiting patiently nearby as I attend to different chapels and saints. The chapel and statue of the Virgin Mary, dressed in her beautiful, soft blue robe edged with white, draws me. She is tenderly cradling her baby in her arms, her head veiled and eyes downcast toward him, transfixed with love and awe. The flickering light of the candles on the altar illuminate her and elaborate gold vases filled with pure white lilies adorn the altar on either side, highlighting the white edging of Mary's robe.

Feeling serene and imbued with the love Mary shows to her boy-child, Christ, I pause, absorbing the natural intimacy of this moment against the backdrop of so much glitter and gold.

I continue walking slowly, placing each foot meditatively in front of the other on the small, square, white-and-black mosaic tiles of the floor. I feel at one with the processional pace and rhythm from observing many liturgical ritual processions during my life. As I circle the interior of the cathedral, with each step, I spiral deeper within my inner being.

I find myself in the center of the cathedral herself and realize I am standing in the center of both my inner and outer worlds.

One of the large, cream-and-gold marble columns patterned with crimson veins draws my eyes. It stands as a sentinel to a life-size statue of Christ. Modern in style, the bronze statue blends with the marble column behind. The ripples of Christ's robe, in darker shades and shadows, stand out as rivers of deep energy drawing me up toward the bearded bronze head, the shoulder-length, wavy hair, and the portion of visible body. The robe is elaborately edged with intricate gold patterns portraying rich embroidery and brocade, as if it were a ceremonial garment of great splendor and high status.

The veins in the marble column behind him mirror and amplify the exposed scarlet heart that is the centerpiece of the statue. My eyes follow Christ's right arm across his chest. His right hand protrudes from under his golden robe, his index finger tenderly reaching out to touch the edge of his heart. His left hand is pulling back his robe, further exposing his heart, as if to show me personally. As I look intently, I feel his heart beating in my body as its crimson color infuses my being. I feel the veins in the marble column transpose themselves through the veins of Christ and into my own body, as the scarlet heart beats and pumps the Christ blood for both of us.

My eyes return to the soft, gentle expression of Christ's face and eyes. They are looking outward across the congregation. I follow his gaze. I see his eyes soften and open as he shows me, through his eyes, what he is seeing and feeling from this commanding position at the center of the cathedral. He watches over the congregation who gather there. Some of the people are in prayer, kneeling, their heads and eyes downcast. Some rest on bended knees but look toward the distant altar. Others just sit, still and quiet in their own worlds of inner reflection. All seem oblivious to each other and to me.

As I merge, inhabiting Christ's body and consciousness, I experience within my own body the sense of the suffering of the people around us who have come to worship. They are praying for love, mercy, understanding, forgiveness, and compassion. I am witnessing, through inhabiting Christ's body, his depth of insight and awareness. He sees and feels each person with love and compassion. I have a sense of knowing about the steady, gentle equanimity of openness and non-judgmental understanding that he offers to each person.

Moving six feet sideways to my right, but still in front of the statue, I check to see if I was imagining what had happened. Christ's eyes follow me lovingly and, still alive, still joined, we again look out across the people. Some are close, just behind me. Moving makes no difference to what I am seeing, feeling, and knowing. The aliveness and details of the vision transport me into more powerful, ecstatic fields of consciousness as my heart quickens and my body tingles with the intensifying energetic connection and sensual arousal.

I gently wave my hand at Mattias, who has been standing patiently against the cathedral wall next to the doors that lead to the outside world. I invite him to come and stand beside me. As he does, I point to the statue of Christ.

"Please, look, what do you see?" I ask simply.

He obliges me and looks, in a casual way, toward the statue, obviously wondering why I am asking. He immediately glances back at me in surprise, his body jerking, his head pulling back and his eyes widening as he holds my gaze in an unspoken, quizzical manner.

I move six feet back to where I had stood originally and again wave companionably to Mattias to come and stand beside me, pointing to the statue whilst looking up at it myself. Mattias obliges and quickly follows my eyes toward the statue once again. But this time, he seems overcome.

Turning back toward me with an expression of shock across his face, Mattias' mouth drops open, his eyes wide apart in fright, and his chest heaves as he gulps in deep breaths. Without saying anything, he runs for the doors next to where he had been casually leaning only a few minutes before and disappears outside.

I continue to linger in front of Christ, absorbing more of the vision, the embodied connection, and the expansive awareness of unity that I see through his alive, gentle, and soft eyes of compassion. My right hand instinctively moves to my chest where, nestling against my heart, is my new, penny-size amulet of rough, deep brown ayahuasca wood strung on a necklace of small, round, black and red native seeds. My Peruvian *maestros* gave me the necklace as a talisman and link to my ayahuasca spiritual healing ceremonies.

As I gently finger my necklace, I mirror, heart to heart, a mystical union of spiritual talismans, Christian and indigenous. It is a cosmic unity that crosses all boundaries and infuses me with a universal spirit and love. I stand subsumed in awe, not wanting to move. This moment is so perfect, so serene, yet so powerful in its simplicity and directness.

Gradually, I begin to return to my ordinary consciousness. I think of Mattias, alone outside. Reluctantly and tearfully, I bow. With prayers of gratitude to Christ, I bid farewell.

As I step out into the bright sunshine, I am still feeling a little bit in both worlds. Mattias is waiting patiently for me. He now looks far less frightened, but more subdued than he'd been during our early, lively conversations.

"How are you feeling?" I ask him.

"Good," he replies, but I can see that he still seems shocked and overwhelmed. "I know from personal experience the power of spiritual energy, spiritual healing, and working with people's etheric bodies. But to experience the spiritual power from a statue coming to life in front of me, especially when I'm not expecting this, really shocked me. It was so real and strong. I had no time to think about what I experienced when you asked me to come and stand next to you. It was an immediate engagement, like stepping into a movie. The face was alive, moving. Everything was so real. When you asked me to move and look again, the same things happened. I panicked—but I know it wasn't evil. It felt sublime, from another world."

"I saw it too," I say.

I reassure Mattias that even though it was a powerful and unexpected experience, we both saw and felt a similar aliveness and transpersonal energy. For me, it included love. This had been special to me, a privilege and sacred honor.

Mattias relaxes his body and smiles again.

"I didn't feel any negative energy," he says. "It was simply awe that I could feel such an energy field unexpectedly."

He points out that this experience happened specifically for us in a time and place within an ordinary tour of the cathedral, with other people oblivious to it.

Mattias accompanies me back to my hotel and we return to our separate lives, both changed forever. What happened that day with Christ, looking through his eyes and heart, continues to remain fresh, alive, and present with me. It has become a fully embodied experience, always reminding me to shift from my head to my heart—because that is where love, compassion, and healing dwell.

Debbie Irvine, MCoun

HOLDING HANDS IN THE PANDEMIC

I stood under the hot shower in my tiny bathroom, unable to relax. Like everyone else, I felt lonely and worried during the Covid-19 quarantine. *What is this new virus all about? Will the people I love survive it?*

In my town, restaurants had locked their doors. People skipped their usual holiday celebrations to stay indoors, and the streets were empty … except for the snow.

The energy surrounding me became very still and I sensed a private bubble forming around my space. My focus shifted from casual meanderings to deep emotions arising as an inner vision washed over me. I immediately relaxed into the familiar, high energy of talking with Spirit; nothing else was in my awareness now—no shower, no bathroom, no snow, no worries.

My insights were both instantaneous and timeless. Though the actual time elapsed couldn't have been more than a minute or two, I began experiencing people and events from the past, through the present, and into the future.

My cozy house in Colorado disappeared as my awareness traveled to the ghettos in Europe at the beginning of World War II. I was right there, sharing the heavy despair of the people quarantined behind those walls, shut off from a world in which they had been active and productive, left to pace in their isolated enclosure. I shared their sadness as I longed to rid them of their despair. I paused to take a deep breath and open my heart wide to energetically hug each one as they collectively cried: *What's happening? What will become of us? Why are they imprisoning us like this?*

My vision then followed these souls to concentration camps in Germany. I observed lines of men, women, and children; their captors were separating them again into smaller groups. I saw the bleak buildings with bars on the entryways; the lifeless, gray sky matched the fears of the people as soldiers ordered them about. Their confusion was palpable, and I felt my heart begin to close, because it wanted to protect me from the indescribable pain.

Watching the dark scenario, my mind was whirling with questions. *How could such a situation take place? What prompted such hatred and disregard for human life to grow in the minds of their captors?*

My focus shifted like a camera moving to record a new scene. I saw sick people with no chance of improvement, and I clearly felt in my own gut the hopelessness and pain during the pandemic of 1918, more than a hundred years ago. Then, in another flash, I saw conglomerates of wars and abuse throughout our human history.

Is this our legacy? What must we do to stop such heartache?

Immediately following that question, I became conscious of present times. I felt the pain and isolation in multitudes of people around the globe. I had mental images of families in refugee camps and immigration lockdowns as well as long-term residents stripped of their freedom by greedy governments. In a split-second, I viewed religious wars, political wars, and crashing economies and democracies being swept under the rug of lies and deception. All the while, human ignorance and selfishness ignored the continuing misery.

Instantly I grasped that this viral pandemic of my own time was a metaphor for the separateness and hate that we, as a whole, had allowed to seep into the hidden corners of our hearts. I questioned our ability to stop the march of the debilitating virus.

If history is once again repeating itself, is it even possible to seize this opportunity and make new, healthy choices?

And with this question, my vision shifted yet again. Still standing in the steam of the shower, I drew my hands together and interlaced my fingers. There I was with my spiritual light beaming out, connecting with all our hearts in solidarity. I felt black hands, beige hands, brown hands, all locked together, all connected to beating hearts, all connected in love.

I understood that this vision is our future, if we allow it. I heard that when we honestly open our hearts, we'll see that we are all connected and that our connection is Divine. Spiritual connection has no religion, no nationality, no gender. The energy of real, unconditional love leaves absolutely no room for hatred, despair, or loneliness.

More questions arose: *Is it impossible to change our circumstances, given our present global state of affairs? Do we want to return to "normal," or can we globally shift to a new everyday paradigm of compassion and caring?*

My highly focused energy began to wane, and my visions slowed down. This powerful experience ended with a simple and powerful visualization and these words:

Stop for just one minute every day. Breathe in deeply and feel the energy of your heart opening. Breathe out slowly and feel your loving energy moving out beyond space and time through your fingertips. Interlace your fingers and imagine that you are connecting with all other loving beings. Breathe deeply again into this connection.

Let us work together. We can indeed change the world, collectively, one person at a time.

Ronna Webb

THE GOLDEN ROAD

*I*s it true that we forget our true nature when we are born—or are the veils only a game we play so we can have new challenges and experiences?

I find myself walking upon a golden road. It is a road that seems both familiar and strange. Something is striking about my surroundings. The road is made of materials common to an older township road. Larger stones line the edges, and a winding path fills the center. I see only vast expanses of gold around the road. I know the destination is a beautiful place to journey.

I realize what makes this scene so unusual: There are no shadows here. Everything seems to shine from a light within. Light emanates from each stone I see along the path. Every particle seems to exhale light. This is a heavenly road. After many challenges and rites of passage I walk freely, unencumbered by the pulls of the material realm. I feel light and free.

I meet someone who looks like a spiritual teacher along the road. I have not adorned myself in heavenly garments. I must look like I belong somewhere else, I think.

I return to my material awareness and the meditation ends.

I was born into an impoverished home fraught with addictions, and I struggled through every year. Searching for validation and healing from traumas in a dysfunctional way led to a series of wayward relationships that consumed me fully. Without an inherent sense of self-worth, the sorrows of the world threatened to drown me. I felt like Atreyu, hero of the *NeverEnding Story*, losing his trusted steed and companion in the swamps of despair.

I was losing myself. In a moment of surrender and tears, I cried a prayer to the universe. I had no idea if any consciousness truly existed out there. If there was a higher power, how could they allow such sorrow? But the prayer came from my inner depths.

Help me. I need help.

Instantly, I felt relief. I felt that someone had heard me. Angels? Mother Nature? God or Goddess? I could not know, but serenity washed over me. Soon after, doors began opening, and I entered an ashram-styled healing program. It was an unexpected path, but one that began to nourish the soul I had long ignored.

I began to learn a myriad of spiritual things, novel words and lingo, and new modes of behavior. Some were helpful, some not so helpful. I began a phase of deep, inner reflection based on meditation, journaling, and yoga. This lasted many years as I worked to untangle from the destructive habits I had learned in the world. I needed to understand how I ended up in such darkness. Most importantly, I felt a longing to recover the love I sensed I was missing.

I saw love in all of nature, in the trees and oceans, the birds and stars. It seemed clear to me that some organizational force existed and operated out of love. However, I didn't feel loved.

I did begin to feel more optimistic. As I learned through my practice, I transformed. I began to believe my quest was not futile. I experienced many moments of peace and wisdom. I could sense the angels and spirits of nature assisting me. I could feel my kundalini awakening, and my dream states became more vivid. Due to the chaotic and devastating events of my early life, my life-force energy and energy body were empty, perhaps even broken.

My chakras were weak and blocked—my wings, demolished. I could still have spiritual experiences, but when it came to worldly things, I felt angst and pain. I could not fly into a better way of living.

In a dream, I looked into a large mirror and did not see a face I recognized; instead, the mirror reflected a tragic image. I saw an angelic light being whose wings had become torn and broken from the exploitation I had experienced. I was a bird who could not fly home.

Hopelessness came in and out of my mind like a dark cloud. I felt every storm was a huge burden. However, a voice within told me to keep going, even when all was dark. After an experience with some indigenous elders, I began to view the Earth as a place where souls could heal and mend if they ever fell into darker planes. I began to let nature guide me. In the mountains, I found peace. I felt strength in the trees. When I meditated by the river, she received my prayers. She led me to many unusual places, and I often wondered whether this was a real path at all or just a fantasy that might lead me astray.

One day I found myself unable to sit still in meditation. I felt such great discomfort. My kundalini energy was clearly active, but there were no pretty visions, just a feeling that I might be seriously sick. I took myself to a special place near a small waterfall. I rinsed my forehead chakra and gazed into the water. I could see rainbows glittering in the misty pool. I observed a vision of myself birthing a new soul energy. I saw a crystalline egg emerge from my womb; it expanded into a lovely energy infusing all my chakras. I felt my new wings open gently. This was a re-birth and activation.

I understood the Soul of the Earth Mother saying, "I love You. In eternity, there is nothing lost."

Back in my normal life, evidence of the shift became apparent. I returned to a city that I loved, found hope in relationships, and began to see myself with new eyes. I could achieve my goals, which had seemed so maddeningly impossible before. The Earth gave me new life, but it didn't happen overnight.

Many times, during that process, I felt sick and abandoned. It seemed easier to do what the world was demanding, but I knew where that led me. These ideas still pull at me.

But I had struck a magical path, a special journey of awakening. I saw my spirit in all its grandeur infusing this new soul vehicle with life and wisdom. In my meditations, I could now access the golden road.

Anastasia Michelle

BEING LIGHT

a calling, felt deeply in the heart, whispers its sweetness.

Come to me, hold my hand, and let me lead the way. Surrender all your stories and recreate yourself anew. You have a higher purpose of service for humanity and Mother Gaia. Ascension is the doorway. Open to who you truly are; let the codes flow through you and anchor them in. Walk barefoot as your higher god avatar self, as ascension happens here in this embodiment of New Earth.

I was on my journey of self-discovery when I received an email. A group of friends who I offered healings with were heading to India. Leaving in three weeks. A feeling of pure delight flowed through every cell of my body, a joyful dance. The money wasn't there; however, I knew I was going to go.

Divinely guided, I was soon aboard a plane embarking on a quest of awakening. We expected to be there for four weeks, to immerse in experiences of high consciousness. Each day we were up at four o'clock in the morning and finishing with the main session for the day in the temple around nine o'clock at night. For the entire day, the energy kept building up for the last session. Within the incredible essence of this magnificent being, the temple, these final sessions were always deep and profound.

There was a lot to endure, a lot to experience, and a lot to just allow and let happen. My heart was open and my mind at rest. All my senses felt intensified. Without expectations or attachments to what would be revealed, I simply opened to receive the grace of Source in whatever way it wished to express itself, in every moment.

In the evenings, we would travel on a bus for about ten minutes and gather at the front of the temple. We chanted a mantra while walking up and around the temple. Inside, we circled the Sri Yantra, carved in marble, eleven times. As always, the energy was high and loving.

For some reason, one night, I didn't hear what meditation we would do when in the temple. A pulsing of energy was flowing through me as my body and breath were activated. The pulse was so strong, I couldn't chant aloud or even hold my hands in prayer position above my head. Walking with everyone and internally chanting, I made my way to a seat inside. I took a chair, although I usually sat on the floor.

We held hands as the *dasa*, our teacher gave instructions for our meditation. To the left of me was a friend from New Zealand, and on the right was a Chinese lady I didn't know. I felt held, safe, and fully supported. As we were about to start the meditation, I realized what was happening. The kundalini was uncurling and ready to rise.

Our meditation was an intense breath meditation through the chakras, calling the kundalini to awaken. I had done this before with a large group, and I'd become scared of the intensity and stopped the process. This time, in this pure, Divine temple, with a group of about eighty people holding hands, I was ready.

I surrendered to the process with the highest intention of fully opening to the possibility of a kundalini awakening. With each chakra, we were chanting a sound vibration, then calling the kundalini to rise. With the colors of each chakra, and the gold liquid of the kundalini energy visualized, my body was pulsating, rocking, and swaying with each breath. My hands held tight and supported, I was going beyond the physical. My hands rose above my head. My chest was open as I looked skyward.

Then I was flying forward, my head almost hitting my knees. And back again. I bent repeatedly, trying to stay present with each breath, each chant, and intently saying, "Go deeper, go further. Open fully to awaken."

I could barely stay in my chair as I was so aware of my body. And then it happened. As we reached the third eye chakra, everything went still.

A vast ocean of pure, white light surrounded me like a sheet of purity. It felt like love, like nothing I'd experienced before. I could see 360 degrees for eternity. In this nothingness was everything that existed—an indescribable emptiness that was so full of unconditional love. No time or space. No feeling or emotion. No title or conclusion. There I was, so pure. I was watching it all while being it all.

A screen suddenly appeared, like a big TV screen with no edges. On this screen was me, seen in profile. My image bent forward, paused for a moment, and flew backwards off the screen. It was as if I had a big rubber band around my waist and, when I got to full stretch, I was gone.

I had an awareness I was witnessing the old stories and versions of myself that no longer served me. This happened about twenty times. I felt lighter. Once this had finished, many masters appeared, one after another. They approached me from the vast, pure light and spoke wisdom as they moved through my being. I felt soaked in Divine grace and a knowing of the Divine being I am.

Again, a pause. While being immersed in this light, some moments passed. Looking and feeling into this space, far in the distance, higher than this sea of light, an even brighter light appeared. It shone down as I looked on in wonder and amazement. The light pulled me in and, at what seemed like the bottom, I found myself.

I was looking at myself standing in this light. I watched little me floating up toward where the bright light was shining. I felt confused, thinking, *What's happening, what's going on? Is this Heaven? Am I heading to the light?*

As I watched myself slowly head up toward this light, I thought about my life on Earth. I thought about my partner, my parents, family, and friends. I felt nothing, not a single emotion. I was heading to the light, and all there was within me was bliss and gratitude for the life I have lived and all those who were a part of it. Even though I didn't know it before, in this moment, I was ready to go.

Happy and content, I continued to watch as I headed higher into the light. I watched and was almost unable to see myself as this magnificent bright light engulfed me. As I felt myself fully surrender and was about to disappear—suddenly, I was back in my body. Back in the temple, swaying forward and back intensely. Holding the hands of the same people as before, barely able to breathe.

When the meditation finished, everyone got up to dance and celebrate their journey of the kundalini rising. Blissing out in a state of higher consciousness kept me in my chair. The Chinese lady that had been sitting on my right thanked me dearly for having the willingness to go so far. Others came and gave me a hug and blessings. After a while, it was time to get back on the bus. Walking wasn't easy, so two people came to help.

As we walked out of the temple, we passed a drinking tap. The New Zealand lady who had sat to my left came by and said it would be good to pour some water over my head. I couldn't speak, but a voice inside of me said, *Really?* It wasn't good. I hissed like a snake and my body swayed vigorously. Now, I really couldn't walk. Friends carried me to the bus.

On arrival at the campus, I asked my body, *Bed or dining hall?* Immediately I had a hunger pain in my stomach. Then a loud voice inside me said, *Chocolate!*

What? Chocolate?

My friends helped me to a dining hall table, and someone got some cooked food for me. It was a typical Indian food hall with traditional Indian food. It also had a café for us westerners. I had ordered hot chips some days earlier, when the cooker suddenly broke. They had asked me to return for the chips later. This night, the Indian man from the cafe came over to tell me the cooker was still not working.

"But if you would like, for the same price, I will bring you some chocolate."

The Divine was working her magic. After the meal and chocolate, I felt more in my body. I had seen other people have kundalini experiences, and they took days to recover. I planned to go to the sacred mountain in the morning to be of service to others; I was determined that I would make it. I could slowly walk, and as I made my way to the dorm, a guy came up to me.

"Do you remember the beautiful words you said to Mel the other day?" he asked. "Well, she would like to give you something to say thank you."

He put his hand in his pocket and out came some chocolate. I walked to the dorm feeling amused and grateful. Soon after, when one of the guys from my dorm and I were talking, he said, "I have something for you. I put it under your pillow." Yes, it was chocolate.

I made it to the sacred mountain the next morning. I also made it to serve as a conduit for the light to flow through me and to assist others with their journey of ascension and the unfoldment of New Earth.

Jacob Melchizedek

DYING ON THE GARDEN CITY FLYER

For several years, my only spiritual practice was simple: I prayed for at-onement with the Creator through the gift of Divine Love. One spring weekday morning, I sat in the dark in my living room praying intently for the inflowing of Divine Essence into my being. I kept my focus on my longing for God's gift of Grace—as if my life depended on it—for thirty-five minutes.

My typical experience when I prayed for the inflowing of Source's substance was a gentle and pleasant, warming sensation in the area around my physical and spiritual heart. Prayer usually provided a temporary respite from the anxieties and judgments that ruled the rest of my waking hours. During these prayers and shortly after, I often felt at peace and sometimes even joyful. Not today.

After praying with intense desire, I didn't experience the warmth in my chest. I felt no residue of peace or joy—just exhaustion. I felt saddened and confused by the absence of the usual signs that suggested my prayer practice was effective. I was even a little bit miffed at God. I had prayed so hard but received none of the usual blessings.

I didn't have time to wallow in disappointment. I continued my morning routine and walked in the dark to the bus stop to take the Garden City Flyer into Wilkinsburg. It was time to start the journey to my office in the city, where I worked as a data manager and analyst. I got on the bus in the early morning half-light, just before the sun appeared.

As I sat in silence on the bus, I felt a "hot spot" inside my chest to the left of my heart, an intense, hot liquid spurting in my chest. I feared an aortic aneurysm—not that I knew what that would feel like.

Heat began to spread throughout my thorax in all directions. I thought, *My chest cavity is filling up with blood that is leaking from my burst aorta. I am dying.*

I wasn't even thirty years old yet. Why was I having a deadly cardiac event? There had been no warning signs. I had felt fine until that moment. But that's how these things happened sometimes. I expected my body to slump to the side before the inevitable fade to black. *There is no one in the seats on either side of me. Good. I won't fall on anyone. That would be rude and embarrassing.*

I hoped the people on the bus would notice that I had dropped dead, when the time came.

I was at peace. That made sense. People in near-death experiences often described a sense of peace as they're dying. I glanced around at the other bus passengers, who were sitting with their eyes closed, letting the bus's motion jostle them. A couple of them were reading books. There was no point in causing a scene. I allowed myself to die.

But I didn't die. I remained upright. I felt no pain. The intense heat moved into my extremities. Sensations of peace and joy continued to radiate throughout my being, even as my mind was racing to understand what was happening.

It finally dawned on me that I was having a spiritual experience—not a medical emergency. With this realization, I allowed myself to bask in the warmth that was suffusing my being. I had asked for an inflowing of Divine Essence, and I was receiving it.

As soon as the warmth had filled every particle of my body, I started to feel an enjoyable, sparkling sensation in my toes. This fresh and effervescent energy moved up through my feet and legs and continued up through my torso.

I looked around at the other riders, who appeared unaware of what was happening. The Divine freshness continued to move through my limbs, neck, and head. The atmosphere of my being was permeated with delight and wonder—yet my appearance hadn't changed. None of the other riders seemed to notice.

Suddenly I wanted people to know what was happening but didn't see a way to share it. I stayed in my seat, even though my soul was so excited and joyful at what was happening. My body felt like a blissful wintergreen Lifesaver candy dissolving in God's mouth.

As these bright, sparkling sensations faded, deep waves of gratitude brought tears to my eyes. I blotted my eyes as the bus arrived at my stop.

It was a different man—not dead, but transformed—who got up from the seat, stepped off the bus, and crossed the street to go to work.

Bill Frase

MY LIGHTBODY REUNION

Once I'd had a glimpse of eternity, it was hard coming back to the present.

Three or four days after my father passed, I had a deeply transformative experience. In this vivid dream or vision, I felt and saw my father before me as his light essence. He invited me—in unspoken word-thoughts—to come with him.

Taking the form of my own lightbody, I joined my father on an astral travel journey, playing and romping throughout the galaxies. As light essences, we merged, separated, went anywhere and everywhere, and experienced being anything and everything—as well as being nothing. Sometimes we paused, indefinitely, and other times we zoomed from place to place at light speed. At times, our perspective was all-seeing and all-knowing. Other times, we occupied an infinitesimally tiny space deep within an atom, and we had the perspective of the tiniest possible vantage point.

Together, we explored the past, the present, and the future, all as one continuum. Within this span, we could see and know everything as if it were here and now, in one indistinguishable ever-moment. We traveled through countless dimensions, each having its own flavors and colors and its own set of realities and beings. We enjoyed the experience of trying on each one.

Time felt never-ending in each boundless moment. Our being-ness was immeasurable in place and time. We were Light Essence, Soul, and Source. We were the creators of All That Is. This adventure was more pleasurable than anything I'd ever felt or imagined, yet I was there, experiencing all of it. My father was there, too, reassuring me and guiding me from one aspect to the next and the next. I felt his intention that I see and sample what he had found in this form after the death of his earthly body.

Eventually, the sheer intensity of the joy that I felt brought me fully awake. My sleeping physical self could no longer contain that immense level of feeling. I was aware that I had made a conscious choice within my dream state to awaken again to life on Earth. Otherwise, I would have perished from the intense joy.

For hours, I lay awake and processed what I had seen and experienced. Even in the moments immediately after the dream, I already felt its clarity slipping from my conscious grasp. I had seen things that no words can describe, and have been saddened that as time passed, I lost the vividness and the experiential glory.

My journey had such depth and wonder, it was far beyond the capacity of the human mind—my finite mind—to create. I believe it was a soul dance of the highest order. I am so grateful to have had that time with my dad. It was a gift and one I shall treasure always.

In the first few days after this experience, I found my perspective of earthly reality had changed completely. I could project myself into other frames of reference, seeing and feeling things from others' perspectives. Sometimes these were human shifts, so I could anticipate what another was feeling and thinking or what they would say. Other times, I could see and experience the world from above, with a bird's-eye view, or from within. I could understand a tree's point of view.

I could feel the life forces around me in new ways: green was a pulsing force in the grass. I could feel love of another in a deeper way, as if there was no distinction between what was "I" and what was "thou." All were one. Some of these perspectives are mine to keep, while others slipped back to their original, more limited-in-me frame of reference.

Vivid, transcendent experiences can be dangerous. Over the following few weeks, I often felt lingering human desire to be in that lightbody state exclusively. With such a strong remembrance of soul, it was often hard to be right here, right now. Strangely, I felt left behind.

As the weeks and months pass, I find pleasure and value in returning to the rapturous feeling and joyful memory of our interstellar, dream-vision journey. Those moments refresh me, raise my consciousness and awareness, and infuse me with peace, healing, and joy.

I can't return to that transcendental form until I have lived as many years as I will be blessed with in this life. But I will be there again. I can wait.

For now, I plan to stay well-anchored to my physical being. I love my simple pleasures, tolerate my few small pains, and have no premature death wish. I cherish my earthly connections to humans and joyously celebrate every heartstring.

Julie Saeger Nierenberg

A VISIT

Meditating every night, right before going to sleep, had brought me beautiful dreams. I felt presences around me, and my healing abilities were opening.

And then one night, I met an archangel.

You never know when Spirit/God/Source will tap in and open your eyes or heart. As a seeker, I had been asking to upgrade my spiritual awareness for the prior ten years. One night, when I was solidly asleep, an extremely bright light in my bedroom awoke me. I could tell that someone else was there. The magnificent, white and gold light was emanating from a large, transparent and resplendent being standing next to my bed.

Immediately I felt their power, their light, and their love for me and for mankind. This reverence and compassion for us was amazing. This angel was beautiful, possibly seven feet tall or so. A halo of Light encircled the head with wings that went way above their head, reaching the ceiling. Orbiting this angelic being were sparkling orbs of Light that felt like Divine, sacred beings. The orbs contained wheels of Light, and eyes of wisdom floated within them. The floating eyes could see within my soul but did not judge me.

The angel looked upon me and we shared information. We spoke and received thought from one another through our hearts.

"I am Gabriel, an Archangel of the One Lord our God. You have called for us and we are here to lift you up in service and in Love."

I sent the thought that I wished to kneel before them. I felt so much love and power in this presence. I did not feel worthy of being in the angel's presence. As I sent out this thought from my heart to theirs, the angel immediately responded:

"You do not kneel before us in adoration. We all only kneel to the Creator, our Source who loves us all, so only kneel to the Creator God as you know. We thank you for your Light and service to the Light...you are receiving a blessing from Source."

In my mind, I was still kneeling before this beautiful archangel who carried so much love and compassion for me and, more importantly, for every person and living creature on the planet. Their love for every one of us was deeper than anything I had ever known.

I felt codes of Light—beams of encoded information—pouring from this being into me. I had no idea what specific information I received, yet felt certain that at some point, I would know or understand certain things. This has happened.

"A final thank-you for your service. Remember, you are never alone. We love you so much. Keep your heart open and receive," I heard the angel say.

Then, like a light switch turning off, my angel was gone. The dark bedroom felt quiet and empty. My body was vibrating, my heart chakra was open, and tears welled up in my eyes. I was lying in bed—but wondered if it was a dream. *Did it have physical manifestation?* Thirty years later, I have not forgotten this visit. I was forever changed by this incredible blessing.

The encoded information from the beams of Light began to turn up shortly after this. My healing abilities grew through training, natural ability, and my increased interest. Suddenly, I learned to channel, and my fascination with all things spiritual and other-worldly intensified.

However, the experience had also taken some things away. I lost interest in many every day, material, worldly pursuits. I left my career for spiritual interests and indulged in sacred site travel, no longer caring what my friends and family thought of the way I was living my life. I became more selective in where and with whom I spent my time, but the connections I formed were deeper than before, although there were fewer of them. By losing interest in the events of the world, I had more time to spend on more spiritual interests. The outward world fell away.

I know many people wish for such an event to happen to them. I certainly had. I believe that anyone who seriously and intentionally connects with the Divine on a committed basis will have a profound spiritual experience.

My angel brought me many changes, including some that were difficult to experience. Yet I remain grateful for the visit and continue to expect mystery and the profoundly personal soul expansion that enhances my soul's journey.

Barbara Ross Greaney

EMERGING THE BEAUTIFUL BUTTERFLY

*T*he beautiful butterfly emerges from its protective cocoon, pumping blood into its unfolding wings, and is gently lifted from its perch to be carried away by the wind. This delicate creature has grown from egg to caterpillar, consuming food and strength along the way. One day, it enfolds itself into a strong fortress as the nourishment feeds its hungry soul. The butterfly awakens to break free of the cocoon, starting life anew. This precious creature, which developed from difficult beginnings, is now free to give back its own form of wisdom and service, nourishing the environment.

When I was nine years old, I woke up. I had been sleeping, in my cocoon, for four years. I could remember little from before, but I do remember playing with my identical twin, just before we turned five. Then she was gone—and so was I.

It was an accident. I have come to feel deep compassion for those who were involved. I now believe that there is no such thing as an accident; every experience is part of a contract our souls create before we come to Earth. All parties know their roles clearly and have agreed to play their part in the event. But then, as we become physical on the earthly plane, we forget the contract—although we will still fulfill its terms.

It was a beautiful spring day. My sister and I rode along with my uncle and his friend on a shopping trip. When we got back to our own driveway, my uncle helped us out of his friend's truck. My five-year-old mind tells me that my sister got down underneath the truck to retrieve a milk bottle that had rolled underneath. In those days, my family had milk delivered to the house. My five-year-old mind also tells me that I said to the men, "Don't move the truck, because Georgia is under the tire."

I don't know the truth behind this, or whether I really said that. The men laughed, thinking it was a joke. The truck moved, and Georgia was gone. My beautiful twin sister lay there, curled up in a ball with blood coming out of her nose and mouth.

In an instant, they rushed her off to the hospital. I ran up the driveway calling for my grandmother, who babysat for us while my parents worked.

"Grammy! Grammy! Georgia's been hit! I think she's dead!" I screamed as I rushed into my grandmother's arms.

Georgia died on the way to the hospital, and I never saw her again. I only remember Gram holding me and crying while I tried to comfort her.

"Everything will be okay, Grammy," I said, patting her back. "I will take care of everything."

And then, I disappeared.

I believe with all my heart that this was the major soul contract in my life, for it impacted my whole view of the world from that point on.

I have no memory of the funeral or any of the surrounding details. I don't remember holidays or much about life for the four years after Georgia died. I was going through the motions of living, but mentally, I was far away. I now realize that I was observing from another plane of existence.

I do remember waking up at nine years old and discovering that I was here on Earth. I found myself outside on a lovely summer day, sitting on my favorite rock in our front yard.

"I'm alive!" I shouted.

What a thrill! I couldn't believe it and pinched myself, feeling pain. Where had I been for so long? An intense feeling of peace surrounded me, and for the first time in my young life, I felt one with the universe. I knew instinctively that Georgia wasn't dead; she was just "over there."

All was well with the world now. Two angels hovered on either side of me, holding me up. They stayed with me until I was about thirteen years old before slowly fading away.

Once I knew I was back in my own body again, I started questioning my purpose here on Earth. What is death? Do we really die? Where do we go when we die? Do we live again? Why are we here?

No one could answer my questions, but my wonderful grandmother came to my rescue with books by prominent spiritual teachers. It was heavy reading for a child, but as my comprehension became clearer, I began to understand the different concepts of life after death. I didn't realize that this information was healing my grief.

I made it my life's mission to seek answers and find out the truth of our human existence on this planet. I devoured books about Eastern and Western philosophies. I read about different religions. I took classes on the "New Thought" movement, whose followers embrace the belief that we create our own universe.

I have come to believe that we are all part of one whole, and nothing separates us from our Source and Creator. My purpose in life now is to develop more love and compassion and keep shining my light.

I am peeking out of my cocoon now as I tell my tale of bereavement and enlightenment. My dear twin sister came here briefly to launch me on this wonderful spiritual journey of truth, and I am grateful.

J. H. Lutz

A RESET

*a*s I sat in my bedroom chatting online with my girlfriend, I suddenly felt that something was squeezing me. The squeeze was not hard— it was actually delicate. But I knew I should lie down on my bed.

As soon as I did, I felt like I was floating upward. I knew I wasn't dreaming, because I could hear the birds chirping outside my window.

When I opened my eyes, a being was standing to my right. I was lying on my back and couldn't move. Yet I didn't feel fear—just curiosity.

"What's going on?" I asked.

In my mind I heard the reply: *Think, think, think.*

What do you desire? It asked me.

Love, peace, and joy. But what is going on? I replied.

We're resetting your heart, the being replied. Then I heard the word "love" repeated three times.

The being continued to give me instructions. *Whatever is going on in life, always think of that which you love! When difficulty arises, think of what you love.*

Suddenly, the being began to send me messages at a lightning-fast pace. I remember complaining, *I can't remember all this that you're saying!*

You will remember it when it's necessary, the being replied.

I blinked my eyes and realized the being had disappeared. I was still lying on my bed, and I couldn't tell how much time had passed. It might have been hours or just a few seconds. I looked around for a minute, but exhaustion overtook me, and I fell asleep.

The next morning, everything felt different. Before this happened, I didn't have any desire to feed the birds and squirrels that I saw in my backyard; now I have three bird feeders and I bring treats to the squirrels every morning. I meditate twice daily and I have become interested in sacred geometry. I have a different perspective on life.

I didn't mention anything about my OBE to my girlfriend, fearing she'd think I had lost my mind. However, when we had our next video chat, she said that I looked somehow different.

"Your eyes have changed," she said. "It feels like you're looking through me."

A few months later, she told me she had seen blue and white orbs outside my bedroom window. I chuckled, because I had seen them, too. As I stood on my deck, I had noticed a nearby tree decorated with what I'd assumed were Christmas ornaments—until the balls of light began to move around.

My life has become an interesting adventure since they reset my heart.

Mark Sakalosky

THE MOON AND ME

On my knees in the darkness by the side of the river, I watched the evidence of my indiscretions float away. I closed my eyes …

My mother called me a wild child. I felt trapped in a cage of rules and schedules; people always pushing and pulling at me, always watching me. That summer, whenever I got a chance, I escaped. I left my childhood behind to find a new reality.

In retrospect, my childhood had been good, except for a few challenges, like a brother two years older and an absent father. My mother traveled all over the interior of British Columbia creating a network for women to sell jewelry through at-home parties. Until Mom could make a home for us, we stayed with my maternal grandparents. My aunt and her two children lived there, too. The four of us kids grew up together.

One day, hormones hit like a Howitzer and my life exploded.

Someone supported me by the river that night, but I had no attention to give them. I noticed only how miserable I felt. Yes, I'd succeeded in changing my reality, but this new one felt distinctly worse than Moms. Chaos reigned in my mind and my stomach threatened to erupt again. I breathed carefully.

Peeking, I saw a bright path before me. My eyes followed the trail across the dark river; blinked at the far shoreline and jumped up to find the source of the reflection. Everything stopped as my eyes came to rest on the face of the full moon. She took my breath away.

I felt a sharp pain. It felt like my heart had ripped free of my chest and thrown itself at the moon. The pain confused me, having no cause I knew. Part of me considered that and wanted to take care of my body; another part was agape at the beauty of the moon.

Help me, I heard.

That was my voice. I hadn't thought to speak. Those words did not come through my brain. Not only was I unaware that I could be helped, but framing the request was beyond me, as I was busy wondering what had just happened. Hearing my words, I realized the prayer was already answered. The storm within me had calmed. I breathed, *Thank you.*

A tendril of thought and the ghost of a smile were born. A rhyme that came to mind amused me—what would "a boon from the moon" cost? Another part of me was aghast. What did I have that the moon would value?

I witnessed my mind, scurrying like a squirrel, searching all the corners of my brain for something, anything... Busy as I was with the search, I was surprised once again as I heard more unplanned words come out of my mouth:

"Yes, I will speak for you. When the time is right, I will speak for you."

I couldn't hear the conversation my soul was having with some Greater Power. I still don't know what name to give the "You" I spoke to. Through the years, I've considered several possibilities: the Moon, Gaia, God/Goddess, the Divine Feminine, or the collective "I" inside everyone.

I've come to enjoy a term that represents my two-way, ongoing conversation with the Divine. I call it Magic in Ordinary Moments or MOM.

To me, these three synchronistic initials inspire an ongoing conversation with the Divine and personify the power that empowers All That Is.

Shannon K. McArthur

CARIUS

*H*aving agreed to send one of my mares and her foal to spend time keeping a new mother and her foal company, I was growing restless, waiting for the barn owner to come and greet us. I ambled slowly down the center aisle. A pair of eyes that looked my way caught my attention and then glanced down. I approached the stall and peeked thru the metal bars. Again, the eyes looked up. The shadows drew heavy, dark lines across a long face and neck.

"Hey," I whispered. "You in there?"

I could see the shadows move as the weight shifted from one hind leg to the other. His head remained low.

"Hey," I repeated.

I noticed a small, cell-like door with a latch and loophole. I reached up and unlatched the door. It couldn't have been more than a two-by-two-foot opening. It looked like one of those openings the warden might slip food through when feeding prisoners. Ah, yes, that was it. This was a fancy, high-end prison for horses. I wondered how many prisoners were in this building.

Reaching my arm through the feeding window into the stall, I hung it down the other side of the wall. I spoke in a low, soothing tone.

"Hey buddy, you want a scratch?"

I heard a soft nicker. He was hesitant, as though trouble might happen should he speak up. He lifted his muzzle very slowly and sniffed my hand.

From my view, all I could see was the top of his poll—the area between the ears and a luxurious, thick patch of mane. I stretched to see along the inside wall. His muscles rippled against a massive frame. This horse was huge. His breath was warm on my hand, and I turned my palm up slightly to touch his muzzle.

He moved in closer. I scratched under his chin. He lifted his head and looked directly into my eyes.

Get me out.

I furrowed my brow. My hand stroked the underside of his jaw. Then I slid my palm over the bridge of his nose.

This magnificent animal inquired again, *Can you get me out?*

I stood there looking into his single, unblinking-demanding eye.

The world can speak to us in many ways. It comes when we least expect it, and sometimes when we really don't want it. This was one of those moments I didn't want. *What could I do for this horse?* This gorgeous, unbelievably well-trained, expensive athlete was asking to be free.

I stood there with my hand on his neck. He moved a step forward and my hand slid onto his shoulder. I knew I shouldn't even be touching him, let alone setting him free. He shifted his weight and lifted his massive head above the stall threshold. Now we were looking into one another's eyes.

"I'll do whatever I can," I mumbled. *What the hell was happening to me?*

The information came fast and furious. I was getting all kinds of "knowing." I felt overwhelmed. I pulled my hand out of the opening and stepped back to take in the sight before me. He still looked directly into my eyes. He didn't flinch.

I reached over and pulled the stall door slightly open. *Heaven help me.* My movements were not my own. My thoughts weren't functioning. I slipped inside the stall with him.

Enormous, he towered above me. I took in the smell of shavings and urine. He moved forward and placed his head directly against my chest. I held his neck on either side.

"I am so sorry," I whispered.

My thoughts continued to race.

I must be here to help. I believed I would not have witnessed this animal's suffering if there was not a way for me to help. *I am breaking the law right now. Oh, God. I will try my best not to let you down. I will try my best for you.*

The sound of truck wheels crunching over gravel rocks sent me sprinting to the outside of the stall.

"I promise, I will be back."

Door closed, latch fastened, I briskly walked to the entrance to meet the woman who owned this facility.

"Come, baby, come!" Beth, the barn owner, was motioning for the filly to follow its mom. I stopped to catch my breath. There are no words created to define the beauty that stood before me. I was speechless. *So this is what imported European Warmblood foals look like?*

"Isn't she something?" Beth said with a smile. "We are so happy you are here. Baby needs company."

I enjoyed the view of this temporary home boasting lots of room for foals to romp. The mares cantered alongside the little ones as they frolicked. I pondered what I had just experienced a moment before. It felt a little odd. *How long do they get to be horses before they go into cages here?*

The owner and I said our goodbyes and I promised to check-in. I silently made a solemn vow to go back and see that horse.

Months passed, and I received the call to retrieve my mare and foal. Arriving intentionally early, I was in a hurry to find the big, dark horse. I looked around. Just as before, the place was like a morgue. I am big on keeping my promises and was looking forward to seeing this big boy. I approached his stall with anticipation, and my stomach sank.

It was empty. There was no trace of him. No nametag on the door, no vet instructions still in the transparent index cardholder tacked to the wall. He was gone. I thought *Oh my God. How will I ever locate this horse?*

I was disappointed with myself for not making a bigger effort. I had waited too long to get back up there. I scolded myself for my transgression and felt sad that I was not able to help. I wanted to complete the promise I'd made. Not knowing where he was, or his circumstances, felt just awful.

I pondered all the various places he could end up. He had been so unhappy. Now, I was unhappy, too. This horrible knot welled up inside of me.

"Are you looking for Carius?" a woman's voice inquired.

I hadn't known his name. The question caught me off-guard, as I felt unsettled anyway, presuming I was alone. "Um, yes, I just wanted to say hello."

"I'm sorry. You just missed him. He left this morning, about eight."

Carius. I had his name. I blurted out, "Do you know where he went? I mean, did he move for good?"

The woman smiled and replied, "Yes, he left for good, but I don't know where."

Now my spirits were really down. *How could I have failed him like this?*

"Thank you," was all I said. I glanced up to find she was already walking away and out of earshot. I smiled a small, weary smile and made my way toward the exit, heading to the pasture where Gen and Margo awaited. They were both coming home.

Many more months passed, and my lingering sadness stayed with me. Pushing it away from my thoughts provided a moments' distraction. I kept telling myself there was absolutely nothing I could do. I became comfortable talking to Spirit about him, asking for the safety and happiness of my giant friend. I was also selfishly asking for a sign.

My daughter Jillian decided it was time for me to have a riding companion of my own, and so our search began. I was looking at rescues, searching for a horse in need of a new home. I came across a lovely thoroughbred living at a prestigious university barn not too far from us. I made an appointment to visit. Jillian and I arrived on a gorgeous, sunny morning.

Rows of horses poked their massive heads into the center aisle to greet us. They were curious to see who we were, as if thinking, "New visitors! Yay, check for treats!" They stretched their necks as far into the center of the aisle as was physically possible. I had to chuckle.

We found the office and introduced ourselves to the manager. A horse we were considering, Jove, was already standing in the crossties.

"Well, hello Jove." He stood obediently and looked into my eyes. *Beautiful boy*, I thought. Vanessa saddled him up and began chatting about all things Jove. When it was time to hop on, I felt inadequate.

Finally, Jillian said in her kindest coaching voice, "Get over it, Mom, you're fine."

I smiled and up I went. And so we began our stroll. Taking care of me like a bodyguard would, Jove carried me around the arena. As we all headed back toward the barn, I was learning all I could about my new boy.

Inside, the barn was full of activity. Someone was teaching a class over in the crossties. In another corner, a couple of cute girls were fussing over their horses, chatting it up. There was a nicker from my left side, and I turned, expecting to see someone leading yet another horse into the aisle way as it stretched for treats. The man, obviously a teacher, rested his hand on this gelding. He had stopped his lecture to inquire about Jove.

"How do you like him?" he asked.

"He's fabulous!" I said, smiling.

"Isn't he? We all love Jove!"

It was in that instant I glanced at the gelding standing quietly. I looked at his eyes and he threw his head up. He nickered and lifted a front hoof. He pawed at the mat underneath.

"Carius?" I inquired.

The man's face lit up as he asked, "You know Carius?"

The sudden appearance of this horse stunned me. I was at a loss for words. Eight children were looking at me, waiting for my reply. I could see their thoughts spinning. *Do you or don't you?*

"Um, kind of, but not very well," I muttered, slopping my way through an answer. I moved toward him.

"Well, he certainly knows you."

Once again, Carius's massive head tucked into my chest. I felt my tears well up, a knot sitting in my throat. This time I heard, *They love me. I am good.*

I stroked his neck and explained to my audience that we had met briefly at his old barn. I told them he seemed much happier living here.

"Really, we were just acquaintances," I explained.

The instructor began sharing just what a fabulous horse Carius is and all the wonderful things the students learn from him. I was smitten with the idea of this magnificent animal having his own fan club. No more lonely hours in a quiet, empty barn. Solitary confinement was over. The giggling girls told tales of warm baths and spa days full of grooming and fussing. A chunky little cherub stepped forward; her face full of freckles.

"I just adore him!" she pronounced.

Her arms supported her excitement as she lifted them high above her head. She was gesturing to me and hugging him at the same time. My heart was full, knowing all was well. Jillian and I entered Vanessa's office to arrange to bring my new boy home.

I now put all the puzzle pieces together. The trip to the fancy dressage barn wasn't about Margo and Genevieve and the stunning filly. It was for Carius and me. I learned that I have to trust and understand that each circumstance reveals its purpose at the right time. It takes my courage and commitment to trust that Spirit holds me in their loving protection, and that I am not alone.

As the afternoon slipped into the early hues of dusk, I could feel myself smiling and thinking to myself, *I can do this. I'll travel to the new unknown, become vulnerable, and ask my physical self to be silent. I will trust my spirit and heart.*

I think my spirit or heart-side is where the breaking down of boundaries begins. Love and understanding live there.

Thank you, Carius, for helping me understand.

Lynn Hummer

THE WORMHOLE DANCE

When the phone rang in my boat cabin, I was hesitant to answer it. After a long but incredibly exciting day, a nap seemed in order and the Nile was gently rocking our boat. Still, I picked up the phone. It was the ship's concierge calling to tell me that everyone was gathering soon to watch the belly dancer performance.

"Sorry," I said, "but I am going to pass."

A few minutes later, he rang again. "William, everyone is wondering where you are. The belly dancer is about to start."

Feeling pressure to join in, I wandered into the ship's lounge. Sinking into the comfy, C-shaped sofa, I ordered a Stella beer and waited for the dancing to begin. Three Egyptian musicians were jamming. With the call of the drum and the colorful keys of glory from an electronic keyboard, suddenly "Benny and the Pyramids" (not their real name) had my feet tapping. They weren't Led Zeppelin, but hey, I thought, they're alright.

Still, I looked around the room filled with the Japanese, Spanish, and German honeymooners, I felt as I had at the junior high dances as a youth; I was looking to make an appearance and then a fast exit before the dancing started and these genuine Detroit goods were pulled onto the dance floor to do my variation of the Motown "Cool Jerk."

It's strange how stupid we can act and how unaware we can be of imminent, life-changing events. Every Ascension-quester knows the feeling. There is a moment, totally unexpected, when the universal onion unseals, the sky opens, the whirlwind appears, or the chariot of the gods manifests. Suddenly, we are in a whole new world, another level.

It's called *synchronicity*. One of the keystones of ascension teachings is the moment when we know a higher power is operating in our lives. Call it our guardian angel, our higher self, or our ascended self—if we say yes to the higher power, wonderful things can happen.

Benny and the Pyramids changed their tune—and then, the synchronicity appeared. Tall. Rail thin. Stoic. The "belly dancer" entered the room, walked to the center, and started to gently spin in place. *Oh great*, I thought. *I came downstairs to watch some guy do a weird dance? What is this? I thought it was going to be a woman dancing.*

There's nothing wrong with guys dancing, but I came to Egypt to see images of resurrected pharaohs ascending upon wormhole-shaped boats.

In that moment, I didn't realize how blissfully and annoyingly unknowing I was—but also, how lucky.

As I watched the dancer, a whirling dervish, I soon found myself picking my jaw up off the floor. He presented a brightly colored, bell-like skirt that spun around his body. It looked like a saucer-shaped UFO spinning around him.

Then he presented a second saucer and spun it around his body. He lifted it above his head. I was ecstatic. I couldn't believe what I was seeing!

With one saucer spinning above his head and the other below his waist, he had formed the shape of a wormhole! The two skirts at the top and bottom of his body were the two mouths of the wormhole. His body was the throat.

He is a dancing wormhole!

Now, I was up and dancing.

He was performing the alchemical transformational process of Ascension, the one I had just spent the past three days lecturing about. The one I had come to the temples of ancient Egypt to explore further.

The whirling *sema* or *same* ceremony of the Divine love and mystical ecstasy is an 800-year old, mystical Islamic dance performed exclusively by dancers from the Al Tanura Group. The dance is known as *al darweesh*, or "dervish" dancing. It begins with the dervish spinning in place. The Persian word *darwish* (literally: "the sill of the door") is accepted in Arabic and Turkish (*dervish*) to describe the Sufi who is at the door to enlightenment. Derived from the Persian word *dar* (door), a dervish is one who is *poor* (*pure?*) in the sight of God and in need of His mercy.

We might say that the dervish is a mystical dancer (the "pure") who stands between or unites the material and cosmic worlds. Through his spinning, he arrives at a place where ego dissolves and achieves a resonance with universal soul. It is believed that the dervish is in prayer and that his body becomes open to receive the energy of God.

Traditionally, the dervishes start by wearing black cloaks symbolizing empty tombs (after the deceased is removed) to remove themselves from the world. The purpose of the ritual whirling is for the dancer to empty himself of all distracting thoughts and place himself in a trance as his body conquers dizziness. He accepts that he is the true instrument of God and therefore he does not question the power that comes and leaves him during the spinning trance.

A special ability of these dancers is the ability to spin in place, in a counter-clockwise circle, for hours, their feet forming a never-changing, intricate pattern. Twenty to thirty times a minute, the dervish twirled for Allah. Adherents believe this tight, circular movement represents the universe, which stems from a single, spinning point. Their twirling is a form of prayer, a method of tapping into hyperconsciousness, and an act of love.

When I talked with the dancer after his performance, he told me the "story" revealed by the dance concerned the unity of heaven and earth. The circle is perhaps the most ancient of mystical symbols and the most universal of all dances. It is the earth and the sun in eternal movement, an unbroken, unbent line symbolizing continuity and eternity. The circle dance represents the wholeness of things, the roundness of pregnancy, the breasts, vessels, egg, and temple. The dance brings life full circle.

I called the performance the "wormhole dance" and began including it in presentations about my theory that the human body was fashioned as an ascension vehicle. Part of what this meant was that the body could be transformed into a wormhole through which the soul could ascend. The ladder to heaven truly is within us.

William Henry

PART THREE

Deepening Your Ascension Experience

I saw the angel in the marble and carved until I set him free.

—MICHELANGELO

SHIFTING TO WHOLE

The three key takeaways, the golden nuggets, of the early ascension stories we explored are these:

- **One**, human souls can attain a higher state of being. In fact, our bodies might have been designed for Ascension.
- **Two**, Ascension is equated with wholeness and holiness. We know we are ascending when we are doing holier things. On an individual soul level, it means raising from the human to the cosmic or angelic realms. On the planetary level, it is a raising of our collective consciousness from I/Earth/Humanity to We/Cosmic/Galactic Family.
- **Three**, these stories told me that we can, and must, plan to ascend.

Many readers probably have a health plan, a career plan, a financial plan, and a family plan—but what about a plan for (y)our soul's evolution? The awakened and ascending soul asks: *What is my ascension plan? How will I get home?* Anyone contemplating or working on these questions is probably an ascending soul.

Stories that inspire us to think about the body as an ascension vehicle are actually calls to Ascension and mind maps for doing so.

If we wish to be an ascended being, we must act like one. The ascension stories of the ancients are meant to help us get our act together.

One figure who I briefly mentioned is the Sumerian hero named Gilgamesh. Most historians concur that Gilgamesh was a historical king who ruled the Sumerian city-state of Uruk at some point between 2800 and 2500 B.C. An archaic inscription from Ur reads, "Gilgameš is the one whom Utu has selected." The Tummal inscription, c. 1953 to 1920 B.C., credits Gilgamesh with rebuilding the walls of Uruk on its antediluvian foundations. By following his metaphysical story in more detail, I discovered a way we can deepen our own ascension experiences.

The *Epic of Gilgamesh* is the world's second oldest story, after the *Ascension of Inanna*. In it, we learn of his meeting with a figure who survived a great flood sent by the gods to punish humanity. This mortal survived by building a great ship or craft. Just like Noah in the later story found in Genesis, Utnapishtim gathered animals into his craft and saved them from the flood. Afterwards, he released the animals to repopulate the Earth, and he and his wife were deified and blessed with immortality by Enki for this act of compassion. Utnaphishtim directed Gilgamesh to a plant that would assure his immortality and Ascension. Unfortunately, a serpent stole the magic plant from Gilgamesh on his journey back to Earth, and Gilgamesh was forced to accept his mortality by the end of the epic.

In the *Epic*, we learn that Gilgamesh was born two-thirds Divine and one-third human. His father was a human named Lugalbanda and his mother a holy being named Ninsun. He is a composite being—perhaps a hybrid, even.

I interpreted this to mean that humans have three parts. If Gilgamesh wants to make it through the (star)gate of the gods, and attain immortality, he will have to clean up his act and put all his parts together. For if he tries to go through the gate only two-thirds whole, holy, or complete the result will not be pretty. It will be like walking into a blender (or a flashing, flaming sword, like the one guarding the gate to Eden in Genesis).

Gilgamesh, like all of us, must resolve his out-of-shape status and become whole (holy) or complete (360) before venturing into the (star) gate to heaven.

Now, because it provides perfect balance with the Divine ruler at the center, divinity/holiness/wholeness is symbolized by a circle with a dot in the center. The Egyptians were among the first cultures to use the circle to represent perfection. The circle with a dot is also the hieroglyph for light and gold.

Thanks to the sexagesimal system used by the ancient Sumerians, a circle is 360 degrees in circumference. Two-thirds of 360 degrees is 240. Gilgamesh's goal is to raise from 240 to 360.

I began to wonder if this story is saying that 240 is the base starting place (let's call it the base "frequency" or "vibration") of all humanity. In ascension circles, people frequently talk about "raising their vibration" or "shifting their frequency." Often, there is a lack of clarity about what this frequency is and how we know we have raised it. How *do* we measure our ascension frequency? That is a very important question.

If we use Gilgamesh's story as a scale, we can now determine where we are on our ascension path. We are somewhere between 240 and 360.

One thing is clear: Our goal is the same as it was for Gilgamesh 4,500 years ago: to raise ourselves from 240 to 360, or from two-thirds to fully Divine, and to shape ourselves into a perfect whole…in order to enter into the exalted circle of those who have ascended and reached a state beyond human.

Let's talk about the circle for a moment, and then circle back to Gilgamesh.

The round shape of the circle, O, is a *ring*. The multiple levels of interpretation of this word offer further insight into how we transit to the next higher *rung* of our ascension ladder.

When we move all the way around something, we make a *ring* around it.

A *ring* is also a tone or a vibration. If we raise or tune our vibration high enough, we are called an angel. We get a halo, a *ring* of light around our head or body.

A *ring* is a symbol of loving connection. When we commit to someone in marriage, we do so by exchanging rings as tokens of our love and devotion.

A *ring* is also a group of people who share a common goal.

When something "rings a bell," we remember it. We bring it back. We reconnect. Adjusting our ring, our tone, helps us to remember the true self. We are no longer disconnected, cut-off, decoupled from our ascended self.

Finally, a ring is a circular or spiral course, like a labyrinth, which is another ancient symbol of wholeness. In the labyrinth, the imagery and symbolism of the circle and spiral combine into a meandering journey that takes you round and round until, eventually, you find the center. Exiting the labyrinth is a symbol of rebirth. Like the labyrinth, the ascension path becomes purposeful once one has awakened to its course.

Think about how different the view is when you are in the labyrinth at ground level and when you are looking at it from above.

At ground level, one can become confused, frustrated, lost. When viewed from above, suddenly the course, including the entrance and exit, is revealed. The labyrinth becomes a beautiful, symmetrical work of art like your completed soul.

All of these levels of interpretation of the word *ring* can also be applied to the word *Ascension*, which is a never-ending spiral of life in which we increasingly raise our vibration and embrace an always-expanding and resonating universe. Ring that in red.

Imagine what your life would be like if you had the intelligence and compassion of an angel. Imagine if you knew your life never ends, but continues on an eternal spiral. What goals would you have? What would you be doing differently?

The question of the ages is: How do we accomplish this? How do we change our ring tone? How do we raise our consciousness? How do we ascend?

Back to Gilgamesh.

The short answer is we do this by changing the things we are doing from the lower "frequency" of 240 to the higher frequencies of, say, 290, 300, or 310, for example.

Every day that you are at 240, you are doing certain things mentally, physically, spiritually, and emotionally. These are your habits. These actions are reflective of your belief that you can and cannot do certain things—or will or will not do certain things.

When you pass through 240 and are at these higher frequencies you will be doing new and different things mentally, physically, spiritually, and emotionally than you are presently doing. You will continue doing certain things, but the emphasis will be on new actions aimed at greater wholeness, holiness, and perfection. To ascend, we need to figure out what those new things are…and begin doing them. Then, we will begin ringing at a new frequency.

The *Epic of Gilgamesh* points to the spiritual actions required for Ascension. It makes clear that the ascension journey is as much a journey *within* as it is a journey upward. The way to go outward into space is to go inward into the heart and mind. It is not an easy path.

"Wide is the gate (the *nibiru*) that leads to destruction and narrow is the way that leads to life."

This phrase, first uttered by Gilgamesh in c. 2500 B.C., was as true as when Jesus quoted it verbatim 2,500 years later in Matthew 7:13-14:

"Enter through the narrow gate. For wide is the gate and broad is the road that leads to destruction, and many enter through it. But small is the gate and narrow the road that leads to life, and only a few find it."

As Jesus said a moment later in Matthew 19:24, "And again I say unto you, It is easier for a camel to go through the eye of a needle, than for a rich man to enter into the kingdom of God."

The width of the gate depends on our behavior during life.

SOME PRACTICES YOU CAN DO

What can we do to attain a higher frequency and widen the gap?

What you need to do is individually specific to you. Likely, you already know what some of these things are. They are the things you have been procrastinating on or thinking about doing instead of actually doing them. You will be more whole, holy, and complete once you get them done.

Some of these actions will be perceived as easy, like changing our diet, meditating, and chanting. You could put this book down right now and do any of these things. When you come back to the book, you will be at a higher vibration.

Other actions, like healing, levitation, teleportation, and the illumination of the body, will be perceived to be more difficult.

Every action in alignment with your more whole and holy self brings about a perceptible energetic phenomenon, a shift in frequency. When we think in new ways, it affects the body. Who we are is what we think about, what we mentally rehearse, and what we think and act as.

This is why we need images of our more perfect selves.

SACRED ART MEDITATION

We can practice activating the Light Body by contemplating, meditating, and reflecting on sacred images of beings who have attained the Light Body.

We need to see the way forward. We need a north star in the sky to guide us. To me, images of ascended beings are "north stars." Knowing that these images can hand off the codes for our own Ascension make them even more powerful.

Keep a painting of Buddha, Christ, Mary, or any other master beside your bed. Before you rise in the morning, spend a few minutes connecting mentally, physically, spiritually, and emotionally with that figure. Allow your brain to make those circuits and release the neurochemicals of that experience. Rise from your bed as that person who is linked with that deity, instead of your usual self.

Seeing is believing. "Where the mind goes the biology follows," says Dr. Mario Martinez.

I would modify this to say, "Where the *soul* goes, the biology follows."

Jesus' transfiguration is the preferred icon for this. Images of Christ radiating light activate the cosmic power of our imagination, which yogic traditions says is a substantial part of the light body. We aren't just using our imagination, however. Neuroscience says that each time we look at an icon of Christ radiating light, a part of us is mirroring his action.

Jesus told the disciples: "Rise and do not be afraid." In other words, raise your vibration and experience the flip side of fear, which is love.

Focusing our mind, our awareness, on these images provides a map for our imagination and our brain to make this experience our reality.

Repetition. Repetition. Repetition. Repetition. Repetition. Through repeated connection with the icons, we can—with the help of Christ, Buddha, or Mary—rise above fear and create our new self...in their image.

Then, do the things those deities do. Act with compassion, wisdom, patience, generosity, and love.

SHEDDING

Purifying the light body begins with purifying the physical body. In order to purify the light body, one must be aware of it. Once you are aware, it speaks to you. If you listen, it will tell you what you need to do. Often, this will include diet, physical exercise, chanting, burning incense, prayer, and most powerfully, visualizations. The 5th century Platonist Hierocles describes the importance of purifying the disciple as follows:

"We must take care of the purity relating to our luminous body which the Oracles call "the light vehicle of the soul." Such purity extends to our food, our drink, and to the entire regimen of our mortal body in which the luminous body resides, as it breathes life into the inanimate body and maintains its harmony."

A key takeaway here is to think about all that we do from the perspective of the light body. Try to relate your actions to your eternal self. Are your actions in alignment with this self, or working against it—suppressing your light and blocking your path? What about your thoughts?

On a daily basis, how much of your thought goes into where you are going once you ascend from here, and how you are going to get there? Is the food we consume nourishing to our luminous body? Wait. Is there a light body *diet*? I am not a nutritionist or dietician. However, it is certain that "eating the rainbow" brings light into our bodies. Simply put, this means choosing a wide variety of vibrant-colored plants and vegetables throughout the day and week. Painting your plate with a variety of colorful plants brings phytonutrients that add years to our lives and vibrancy to all that we do.

When people diet, they often say they wish to *shed* a few pounds. This means to lose fat or stored potential energy. This stored energy can be converted into light body energy via a change in your physical routine.

It is quite remarkable how the word *shed* also means to "give off or out." We shed tears and we shed light or wisdom from those tears. When we get rid of undesirable objects or aspects of our life, we also shed. Freeing ourselves of unwanted attachments make us feel lighter and happier. Happy people are healthy people.

Thanks to jazz musicians of the 1950s, guitar players call their instrument an axe. When they practice, they head for the shed and chop wood.

What do you keep in the woodshed?

Wood.

Wood can be thought of as a fibrous organic material—or it can be thought of metaphysically. After earth, air, fire, and water, is the fifth element wood? It is equated with spirit, space-time, and the quintessence. I think of Jesus, the carpenter, as a woodworker or worker of the holy spirit. We, too, can work with wood. All we need is an axe.

The axe is one of the oldest human tools. It has always been a symbol for battle and for work, creation, and destruction. While it divides, it can also unite. Many traditions associate the axe with lightning and attribute cosmic powers to it, like making it rain and bringing abundance. In other words, the axe is a tool of creation and of opening a path to a better way of life (including Ascension). This may be why ancient cultures thought the axe was a gift of the gods.

Apart from a Gibson Les Paul electric guitar, my personal favorite axe is the Minoan double axe or *labrys* due to its distinct, symbolic meaning and sacred symbolism. This perfectly symmetrical, double-sided axe is a powerful symbol of balance. It reminds us that we have two sides to us—male and female, good and bad, light and dark, earthly and heavenly. It reminds us to transcend our duality.

In Crete, the *labrys* is shown over the head of an ox, just between its horns, as a symbol of the *mandorla* or gate of light that leads to the higher worlds and reflecting our need to balance the earthly and the heavenly. It shares the same meaning as the Hindu *vajra* as a symbol of compassion in action and celestial illumination. The *labrys* was a symbol of Crete's Divine feminine culture and was used to invoke Divine protection. It is the origin of the labyrinth (the house of the Double Axe), which represents the journey to the center. This is an important connection, as the labyrinth is often seen as a symbol for the soul's incarnation on Earth.

What do you keep in your shed that you would like to shed?

Regrets? Negative emotions or influences? Axes to grind?

Take inventory. Write them down on paper. Then, one by one, take your spiritual axe to those things. Chop them up into more manageable pieces. As you divide and separate them from your spirit, you unite with your light body. Give them the chop and disconnect from them. Shred them (and your shed along with them) and shed the light that is left. You will see more clearly.

Your axe may be a paintbrush, gardening tool, scalpel, hammer, piano, or any other instrument. Your wood may be canvas, a piece of paper, a computer screen. Open your tool box. Pick up your axe and start chopping. Show off your chops—that palette of special skills that only you possess.

Your axe aligns you with your light body and enables it to shed power, strength, authority, fertility, freedom, creativity, and balance.

Axe-wielders who feed the fire of perfection by chopping wood derive huge earthly benefits following this shedding, including:

- **Better health**. Whole people are happy people. Medically, happy people are healthier. They also live longer, granting one an increased opportunity to achieve the Rainbow Body, which the Tibetans say can be achieved in one lifetime.
- **Protection**. The Gnostics teach that the powers (dictatorial forces, terrestrial and otherwise) cannot see those who are clothed in the perfect light.
- **Prosperity**. The fruits of the Promised Land manifest for the good people.

- **Sacred relationships**. As we achieve wholeness, *all* of our relationships become consciously sacred.

We began our journey by thinking of our soul as a seed or even the acorn that becomes the oak. We planted this seed in the ground of history and as we followed its roots, we watered it with the ascension wisdom of many cultures. Our shoots shot through the ground eventually, producing branches, fruits, and flowers. Now we find our way to the axe, which doesn't sound so pleasant as it suggests decay.

This is why I prefer the Minoan *labrys*. The *labrys* is not just the axe head, which is very much less useful without its component, the handle, rod or wand, which is made from a tree. They go together. The handle symbolizes Aarth, but it also symbolizes the axis, conduit, or ladder to heaven (made of wood). The tree we grow on Earth (symbolizing our actions in life) will one day serve as our conduit to heaven (or, conversely) our journey into the underworld. Our actions—our axe—cuts both ways.

The *labrys* is shaped like a stylized heart, the center of our Divinity. When we draw a heart, we make two spirals or a double spiral. One goes clockwise, the other counterclockwise. Thus the two aspects or dualities of our self are united. Once united, they can ascend. Here we receive the gentle reminder that the heart's activity is Ascension and unity, especially with the Divine. It yearns for reconnection with Source. Just as the heart is the center of our being, so should Ascension be the center of our life.

CAN TRANSHUMANS ASCEND?

*L*isten, I'll tell you a mystery: We will not all sleep, but we will all be changed—in an instant, in the twinkling of an eye, at the last trumpet. "For the trumpet will sound, the dead will be raised imperishable, and we will be changed...." (1 Corinthians 15:51).

In 2002, while completing my book *Cloak of the Illuminati*, which was about the ascension robe of Inanna and other gods, I came upon a report released by the United States National Science Foundation/Commerce Department called "Converging Technologies for Improving Human Performance." This astounding document presented the U.S. government's plans to merge four separate technologies—bits (computers), atoms (nanotechnology), neurons (neuroscience), and genes (DNA)—into one seamless technology aimed at the human body. It told how understanding the brain, and the merger of our biological bodies with technology, would lead to the creation of a new human species and a new Golden Age with wealth hitherto unimaginable. All this would happen by 2035.

"Understanding of the mind and brain will enable the creation of a new species of intelligent machine systems that can generate economic wealth on a scale hitherto unimaginable," said the report. "Within a half-century, intelligent machines might create the wealth needed to provide food, clothing, shelter, education, medical care, a clean environment, and physical and financial security for the entire world population. Intelligent machines may eventually generate the production capacity to support universal prosperity and financial security for all human beings. Thus, the engineering of the mind is much more than the pursuit of scientific curiosity. It is more even than a monumental technological challenge. It is an opportunity to eradicate poverty and usher in the golden age for all humankind."

The report pointed to specific areas of research that may include prosthetics, exoskeletons, cyborgs, human-machine interface, and wearable computer systems. Just as easily as we adapted to wearing eyeglasses, we will also adapt to augmenting our bodies with all manner of prosthetics and technologies. The goal is to build a better soldier, a super soldier, and ultimately, better humans. Accelerating pharmaceutical research was also mentioned as vital to meet the future convergence of these technologies with humanity.

In essence, the U.S. government proposed hacking human evolution to create a new species, a "transhuman" ... to win wars and to make money.

In 2002, I remember thinking how fortunate we were to have thirty-plus years to come to our senses and prevent this from happening or prepare for its emergence. It was then that I also realized that a bifurcation of humanity was coming. Not only was it foreseen—it is *planned.*

What captured my attention most was the talk about creating an exoskeleton for humans. An exoskeleton is a second body. The report was describing the creation of a new skin for soldiers that would enable them to have super strength and physical abilities, powers of regeneration, enhanced cognitive powers, and more. These powers matched the Robe of Light of the ancients. I realized that we were recreating the cloak of the gods.

As a result of augmenting the human body with advanced technologies, we might cure diseases, rejuvenate the body, alter the body's appearance, increase intelligence, attain longevity, connect with any one across the planet, and even migrate to other worlds.

Now, I have nothing against prosthetics or technology for those who need them. These devices are miracles.

However, I do have a problem when governments and corporations want to change the human body for money.

The ultimate aim of some Transhumanists is to replace the "unfinished" and "suffering" human body with a perfected synthetic version of itself. Then, sooner than later, they hope to dispense with the body altogether, escape the confines of the flesh and blood, and live forever as avatars of unlimited capability in a new, digital kingdom spread out on the Earth and ruled by the "new father"—the gods of Silicon Valley.

This is the technological or Transhumanist Ascension.

Fast forward to 2022. Artificial intelligence is literally running our world. From the military to customer service at the big box store, AI is involved.

We are living in the midst of a technological, and evolutionary, change that will fundamentally alter the way humans live for generations to come—perhaps even permanently.

Some are aware this is occurring. Many are not. Some are embracing it. I am not. AI's rapidly growing ability to assimilate data and to beat humans at most games; its ability to watch and understand videos; and its stunning creativity (the images and videos it creates from text descriptions are mind-blowing), have experts warning that we are on the edge of the biggest event in human history: the moment when AI becomes conscious and, possibly, lethal to humans. It most certainly will accelerate past us, say some experts. The consequences would be equally dramatic.

Companies have been cleared for human testing of the "brain/computer interface," a nano-brain implant that enables communication between the human brain and AI.

The human brain has remained unchanged for more than 250,000 years. This is when neuroscientists say the human neocortex—the new part of our brain that makes us all human—was activated by some mysterious force.

Today, we are not only putting a new layer in our brain, but we are also connecting our brains to a new ecosystem, the internet. We are creating a parallel online reality, called the meta reality, and a "meta human," an artificial version of ourselves, into which we will deposit our consciousness, migrate to the parallel "meta" reality, and live forever.

Evidence of this is the pervasiveness of, and our interdependence on, the Internet of Things (the twenty billion-plus and growing "smart" things accessed, managed, and monitored through the Internet) and other technologies that have emerged out of the cloud of human consciousness since the transistor was first invented.

It is not just our electronics, appliances, garage-door openers, security systems, fitness bands, and smart watches that are now strung together in our wired world. We are also weaving our physical bodies, and those of our children, into the Internet of Things, recently rebranded as the Internet of Bodies. Devices that connect the human body to the internet are on the rise and will soon be commonplace.

This is only the beginning.

The *Singularity* describes the imminently approaching time when our exponentially accelerating artificially intelligent machines surpass human intelligence and take on a life and agenda of their own, and we merge with them (or are assimilated).

By definition, singularity refers to a time beyond our comprehension. It is rather like explaining our modern world to an ancient cave-dweller or ice cream to someone who has no sense of taste. There's nothing to compare it to.

Most world governments and all the world's major technology companies are involved in this "techno-ascension." They are competing with one another to attain superiority. To them, trillions is the new billion dollars.

Connections. They are driven to attain singularity before 2035, if not sooner. Though some maintain that AI will eventually kill humanity, they have determined the potential benefits of unleashing AI outweigh the risks. This is not a conspiracy theory. We are living it. We participate in the evolution of AI, and the creation of its ecosystem, every time we go online.

With AI as our new companion, the human future will be unlike anything we have known in the past. Our body, itself, may not even be the same.

The only way to exist in this world will be to merge with AI. Virtual Ascension.

Presently, we are in the transitional 3.5-4D period, as evidenced by the sudden appearance of new, "training wheel" transhuman technologies aimed at transcending mortality, or making us immortal by transforming our flesh and blood bodies into machines with replaceable parts.

With the convergence of artificial intelligence (AI), genetics, neuroscience, virtual-reality technology, accelerated 5G wireless internet, and the Internet of Things, we are entering an era where—like the 4D dream state—all things are possible. We will see this technology take over every aspect of our lives within the next few years. The elite call this the "Fourth Industrial Revolution." It is characterized by the blurring of the lines between our biological bodies and our digital bodies.

With simulated or virtual reality technology, we can travel into the past and into the future. We can fluidly alter our bodies. We can create any kind of creature. Through mind uploading, we will be able to "live" permanently in this fluid, dream-like, simulated reality created by artificially intelligent quantum computers. This is the technological version of Ascension.

A primitive version of this are platforms where users are creating cartoon versions of themselves, called "avatars," to interact with other avatars online. From time to time, developers promise, we may seek to leave this dream world and upload ourselves to a new physical body in the "real" 3-D world.

The risk is that the "souls" living in the fake world would not be fully aware or would forget that they are living in a simulation.

Some mischievous overlord—whether alien or artificial intelligence, let's say—could trap them in this "pit" or new "Garden of Eden" forever. "By the 2030s, virtual reality will be totally realistic and compelling and we will spend most of our time in virtual environments …

… We will all become virtual humans."

Some say they will never get up in one of those things. Actually, most of us already have one foot in this new Atlantis.

When you ordered this book, chances are you did so online via a website. In order for this to happen you negotiated with and agreed to contracts with corporations, governments, and organizations you mostly know nothing about as you conduct your life on the internet. Everything you do is recorded, studied, sold, and stored. On any given day, the average person going about his daily business online is monitored, surveilled, spied on, and tracked in more than twenty different ways by both government and corporate eyes and ears.

In a manner of speaking, the book that you saw on the screen has crossed over the glass from the computer world into physicality.

Most are unaware that they have a "twin" of themself that exists online. This other you negotiates.

Some are begging to take the next step and are creating a physical embodiment, called an avatar, which represents them online. This second you is composed of everything you have ever done online. It will outlive your physical body. Plans call for it to live forever in the online "meta verse," as it is now called. The spiritual implications of this are immense.

In his letters to the people of Corinth, written in the 50s A.D., the apostle Paul asked: "How are the dead raised? With what kind of body do they come?" (1 Corinthians 15:35). Paul warned that if the human body cannot be resurrected, and Christ was not born again…into the rainbow resurrection body, then faith is futile (1 Corinthians 15:16). Paul answered his resurrection question by saying that our physical body is perishable, but is raised imperishable; it is sown in dishonor, it is raised in glory; it is sown in weakness, it is raised in power; it is sown a natural body, it is raised a spiritual body (42-44). And just as we have borne the image of the earthly man, so shall we bear the image of the heavenly man (49).

His questions kickstarted a ferocious, ongoing debate about the resurrection of the human body and its ability to morph into light. When Paul posed these questions nearly 2,000 years ago, he could not have anticipated transhumanism and the "new creatures" and "new bodies" the world is engendering.

Today's spiritual people find themselves in a battle over the human soul, and Paul's words mean more now than ever.

This debate took on a new dynamic in 2020 when a software company was granted a patent that would allow the company to make a chatbot using the personal information of deceased people. The patent describes creating a bot based on the "images, voice data, social media posts, electronic messages," and more personal information. From this data, it would learn how this person thinks and speaks and mimic them in conversation. Users will be able to choose iterations of that person, versions from the age of ten, twenty, forty, or sixty years or derivatives of it. Essentially, this would be a digital clone or reincarnation of the person. This person would now live in the virtual universe. Hence, this is not only a form of resurrection—it is an Ascension, too.

THE SOUL IS A PATTERN

I have spent seventeen years documenting how technology is merging with the human body and warning about what is to come from a spiritual perspective.

What really alarms me is the philosophy behind this technology patent. It is another example of the Transhumanist's mocking or mimicking of spirituality, especially the human soul.

The word "pattern" is bandied about by Transhumanists in reference to the soul. They operate from the principle that your soul is a form encoded in your DNA and in neural networks. To them, the pattern is far more important than the material stuff that constitutes it.

For many Transhumanists, the human "soul" is nothing but a specific program being run on a computing machine called the brain.

Essentially, we are a brain in a vat. To Transhumanists, everything we experience in our (un)real world is simulation and a neural spike. That's it. Period.

The programs that are running in our biological brains can be run—and perhaps even better, they say—in a cyber one.

In the Transhumanist view, your "soul" is just the software that runs the hardware of your body. It is not limited to your current carbon body. Pop this software into other types of hardware (like genetically engineered, super-cyborg bodies, robotic bodies, and energetic bodies made of ones and zeroes) and it will run just fine—or even better.

No matter what they say, even if I could digitally clone myself or my "pattern" and ascend to a virtual or meta reality, it would still not be *me*. This second, soulless me would be doomed to suffering in the knowledge that it is fake. I would live knowing that 100 to 150 years from now I could still be talking about the same things as I do today.

This patent is based on the idea that you, and your "soul," are nothing more than data. It is an update of the philosophy of René Descartes, who in 1650 argued that the human body was a machine. The Frenchman joined a contemporary Englishman, Thomas Hobbes—author of the 1651 book *Leviathan*—as the original mouthpieces for scientific materialism, the religion of the Big Tech Swingers.

Hobbes argued against the existence of such things as the human soul. He was one of the first to describe humans as machines and machine-like.

Religion, especially Christianity, says the last thing you want to do is to lose your soul due to temptation or sin. Hobbes countered this saying, you don't have one to begin with.

What is happening is that, thanks to Transhumanists, a new, patentable, model of human is walking our planet. This being is animated by the belief that their life, who they are, is just information. With every keystroke and every game they play, they are programming or self-constructing themselves. Their life is an artifact in this reality.

The questions that arise are spiritual ones. What will happen to our souls when we become machines or live symbiotically with them? Can Transhumans ascend? Will the machines we are giving life also have souls? Some leading technology companies are proponents of the philosophy that humans can infuse machines with spirit. Does it matter?

Now, it is too late for warnings. My new goal is to provide spiritual guidance to those who do not wish to follow this path of evolution, but wish to remain on the fully human, organic path.

A new version of humanity is emerging, or rather, converging with us. One version of humanity will follow the organic ascension path of what some call the path of *homo neuveau, homo cosmos,* or *homo luminous.* Others may choose the technological path of a next human called Transhumans, H+, or H 2.0. We are the ones who will decide what comes next. While there could be a convergence between technology and spirituality, this would take careful leadership.

MOVING UP

Yes, this future way of living promises earthly fulfillment, longevity, and prosperity. However, there is a deep knowing among many that there is something more beyond all this artificial, technology-enabled joy. We know that the devices that have consumed our lives are just toys (highly addictive ones, too) and the fake versions of ourselves that we create online are just dolls. We also realize that the more high-tech we become, the more it becomes apparent that gaps are appearing between people. Holes are opening within that must be filled. Something is missing. Where did humans ever get the idea to create fake versions of themselves?

This *something* is calling millions of people around the world to spontaneously awaken and actively seek a higher, and earthier (organic), way of living, that simultaneously leads to a purer, spiritual way of living for the benefit of themselves and for the Earth itself. Whether they are practicing yoga, meditation, or other consciousness-expanding activities, they are seeking this *something*. They know that it is found beyond the material world.

That something is wholeness and fulfillment: a sense of love, connection, and completion that toys and technology can never provide.

That is organic ascension. This is what makes our time, and each individual's ascension quest, so vital. We might be the last humans to ascend.

Focusing on what makes us human is where we will find our strength. What is our best quality?

It is to love and to care for one another.

Humans have hopes, dreams, and feelings that machines do not have.

Raising our ascension intelligence, and our humanity, is the antidote to artificial intelligence.

We can never give up. We must always look up. Anything is possible if we

1. Imagine it.
2. Believe it.
3. Live it.

THE BEAMING GARMENT

———— ⊙∕⊙ ————

*W*hat is your Ascension plan?

Organic light-body Ascension? Biohacking/radical Transhumanism? Digital immortality in the Metaverse? Resurrection of the body? Or just death as eternal oblivion?

When it all comes down to it, this simple question is the most important of our entire life.

Never before have humans lived with so many choices. We are fortunate to have been born on Earth as humans, especially at such an amazing, transitional time. Our time is precious. We can spend it on ordinary or mundane things, or we can take this rare and precious opportunity to spiritually perfect ourselves.

Your decision affects everyone and everything you come into contact with.

Choosing the organic light-body path is, of course my preferred ascending path. From a spiritual perspective, human birth is a gift. Billions of people have come and gone on Earth without realizing the full potential of this gift. Presently, nearly eight billion people inhabit this world. How many receive the blessings of this gift and begin to practice Ascension? How many continue to practice? How many reach beyond human to be reborn? Hopefully, as many as there are stars in sky. Just imagine such a world.

It is my hope that this book has brought light, wisdom, insight, history, and, especially, keys to help you along your path. Thank you for reading it and taking this practice forward. Your practice matters. Your story matters.

As a parting word, I would say that, in the end, the next step in your journey is a simple, but powerful one, maybe the most powerful.

If we wish to ascend to a higher reality, as many of us do, we must begin to think, and act like the beings who live there while we are in *our* reality. In other words, we have to think and act as if we already live there, *here*.

And now.

As if it is already a reality.

Now.

Imagine you have already attained your Ascension. What are you seeing? What are you doing? What are you feeling? Bring that feeling into this present moment.

My promise is that as you immerse yourself in this feeling, day after day, month after month, the spiritual qualities of the pure-hearted will develop, removing the veils human existence places upon us and filling your being with light.

The Beaming Garment can be achieved in *this* lifetime. You will wear it. Just believe.

And live. Live for Ascension to live your Ascension.

MEET OUR SACRED STORYTELLERS

SUSIE CASSARO jumped ship in Diego Garcia to escape a drug addiction. She knew things needed to change drastically in her life. After eight years, she came home to Washington, clean, but fearful she would fall back into old habits. Her life has since moved forward into the world of self-help. lightsideofdarkness.com.

JULIA EILER is a Qero Incan Shaman, clairvoyant, and spiritual mentor. She is creator of The Shaman Soulution, with a passion of helping others to step into their divinity through shamanic healing practices. Julia loves helping others to self-discovery, self-empowerment with a focus on discovery and development of their extraordinary gifts. theshamansoulution.com

BILL FRASE is the author of *Soul Fire: Awakening to the Power of Divine Love* and the Wake-Up Call for the Soul blog. He is co-founder of LightBringers. lightbringers.info.

BARBARA ROSS GREANEY is an ordained minister with the Universal Brotherhood who explores spirituality in her writing, meditations, healing work, soul path readings, and channeling. She lives in Leesburg, FL. reverendbarb.com.

YSETTE ROCES GUEVARA, PH.D., gardens in co-creative partnership with Nature in New York's Hudson Valley. She works with humans who wish to find their center, surrender to mystery, and step into mastery. mindsonfire.org.

DR. JOANNE HALVERSON lived off-grid in nature. She has a doctorate in clinical psychology. Traditional Coast Salish Indigenous spiritual leaders (shamans) entrusted her with initiations, wisdom, and medicine names. Such gifts are meant to be shared. Her medicine names are Ancient Spirit Person and Sikahtahlia which means guardian of the earth.

LYNN HUMMER is founder of The Pregnant Mare Recue, Inc. She shares her story of inspiration found in serving others in her memoir *For The Love of Horse* and her series of children's books *Stories From Our Rescue*. pregnantmarerescue.org.

J.J. HURTAK, PH.D., PH.D. AND DESIREE HURTAK, PH.D., are authors and cofounders of The Academy For Future Science, an international NGO that works to bring cooperation between science and local cultures through education with an emphasis on sustainable development. Dr. J.J. Hurtak is the author of *The Book of Knowledge: The Keys of Enoch*´ that details his experience and is also a social scientist and specialist in space law and cosmology. Dr. Desiree Hurtak is an environmentalist, social scientist, and futurist. keysofenoch.org.

DEBBIE IRVINE, MCOUN who resides in Australia, traveled to South and North America for spiritual healings. These mystical experiences healed her permanent primary immunodeficiency disease, critical hypertension, and transformed her life. Previously declared Total and Permanently Disabled with ill-health and retired from her musical career, Debbie now practices as a counselor and a shamanic and dreamwork practitioner.

DONNA KUEBLER is a world traveler and multi-dimensional healer who reads soul records to restore one back to wholeness. She's a channel, seer, shaman, Melchizedek priest and sound healer who shakes the sistrum to help you feel, happy, holy, and at peace. thegoldenalchemist.com.

J. H. LUTZ is a former English teacher and writer. Her spiritual journey began as a small child, and has continued through today, ever-expanding as she develops philosophies along the way.

SHANNON K. MCARTHUR is inspired by being chosen by Gaia to be Her priestess. Creating her role as she lives it, Shannon believes "This is the fun part." ourheartgardens.com.

JACOB MELCHIZEDEK brings about change, be it through his codes, transmissions and activations or self-empowerment and embodiment sessions. Jacob shares the heart is the only place you need to be. jacobbydesign.com.

ANASTASIA MICHELLE is a yoga teacher who is deeply tuned with Gaia. She hopes to inspire those who feel they are ready to step into their soul purpose. alunayoga.wordpress.com.

CLARA STEWART MOORE is a single mother warrior goddess who believes in the magic of the Universe, the power of harmony and the beauty of the truth. She is a global carrier of light and joyfully lives in Brooklyn

New York with her muse and very young composer 13-year-old daughter. radianthealthandwellnessinc.com.

PAMELA NANCE has a graduate degree in cultural anthropology, minor degrees in archaeology and religion, and a 30 year career in social and biostatistical sciences. Pamela has researched the survival of consciousness after death for over 30 years and has obtained certifications in healing touch, past life regression, shamanism and spiritual dowsing. pamelanance.com.

JULIE SAEGER NIERENBERG is an author, artist, and end-of-life educator. She published a memoir about her father's conscious dying experience, and now works to transform how we prepare to die.

MARK SAKOLOSKY didn't believe in anything metaphysical, esoteric, and thought we were alone in the universe before he experienced the event shared in his story.

RONNA WEBB has been in the fields of writing, channeling, counseling and healing for over 40 years. She wrote her first channeled story from Mama in 1986.

SARYON MICHAEL WHITE introduces people to their spiritual guides through channeling and teaches people how to channel for themselves. He is the author of *Roya Sands and the Bridge Between Worlds,* an exciting spiritual fiction novel. saryon.com.

MEET OUR FEATURED AUTHOR

William Henry is a Nashville-based author, investigative mythologist, art historian, and TV presenter. He is an internationally recognized authority on human spiritual potential, transformation and ascension.

He has a unique ability to incorporate historical, religious, spiritual, scientific, archaeological and other forms of such knowledge into factually-based theories and conclusions that provide the layperson with a more in-depth understanding of the profound shift we are actually experiencing in our lifetime.

The spiritual voice and Consulting Producer of the global hit History Channel program, Ancient Aliens, and host of the Gaia TV series The Awakened Soul: The Lost Science of Ascension, and Arcanum, along with his wife, Clare, William Henry is your guide into the transformative sacred science of human ascension.

By bringing to life the ancient stories of ascension through art and gnostic texts, he teaches the secrets of soul transfiguration or metamorphosis and connects people to one another across cultures, time and space. With over 30 years of research distilled into 18 books and numerous video presentations, William's work will guide you to next level of human consciousness and our expanding reality.

William's present work has taken him into the area of transhumanism, which he first began writing about in his 2002 bestseller, *Cloak of the Illuminati*. His latest book, *The Skingularity Is Near: The Next Human, the Perfect Rainbow Light Body and the Technology of Human Transcendence* is a primer and a warning for the looming potential transformation of humanity as we speed closer to meshing computer technology with human flesh.

William discusses transhumanism as the fulfillment of an ancient impulse to transcend our human bodies. His work has propelled him into the role of human rights activist and advisor on the biopolitics of human enhancement as he informs audiences of the unparalleled perils and potentials of Artificial Intelligence and Transhumanism.

Learn more at https://williamhenry.net

Printed in Great Britain
by Amazon